SYMBOLIC COMPUTATION

Artificial Intelligence

Managing Editor: D. W. Loveland
Editors: L. Bolc A. Bundy P. Hayes J. Siekmann

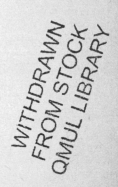

Catalogue of Artificial Intelligence Tools

Edited by Alan Bundy

Springer-Verlag
Berlin Heidelberg New York Tokyo 1984

Editor

Alan Bundy
Department of Artificial Intelligence,
Edinburgh University, Hope Park Square, Meadow Lane
Edinburgh, EH8 9NW/Scotland

Assistant Editor

Lincoln Wallen

ISBN 3-540-13938-9 Springer-Verlag Berlin Heidelberg New York Tokyo
ISBN 0-387-13938-9 Springer-Verlag New York Heidelberg Berlin Tokyo

© Springer-Verlag Berlin Heidelberg 1984
Printed in Germany

Printing: Beltz Offsetdruck, Hemsbach/Bergstr.; Bookbinding: J. Schäffer OHG, Grünstadt
2145/3140-543210

ACKNOWLEDGEMENTS

I would like to thank: the SERC and DoI, who funded the production of this catalogue as part of the Study of Architectures for Intelligent Knowledge-Based Systems; those members of the AI/IKBS community, who wrote the individual entries; the review committee of the catalogue; Robin Boswell, Mike Harris, Luis Jenkins, Mary-Angela Papalaskaris, Dave Plummer, Maarten van Someren and Millie Tupman, who did the low level typing/editing work; John Taylor, for setting up the Architecture Study and for his unflagging enthusiasm and encouragement; Bill Sharpe, for being an ever present source of advice, help and information; and to Lincoln Wallen, who emerged as the coordinator and editorial assistant in a time of need.

Alan Bundy

TABLE OF CONTENTS

PREFACE

The purpose of this catalogue is to promote interaction between members of the AI community. It will do this by announcing the existence of AI techniques and portable software, and acting as a pointer into the literature. Thus the AI community will have access to a common, extensional definition of the field, which will: promote a common terminology, discourage the reinvention of wheels, and act as a clearing house for ideas and software.

The catalogue is a reference work providing a quick guide to the AI tools available for different jobs. It is not intended to be a textbook like the Artificial Intelligence Handbook. It, intentionally, only provides a brief description of each tool, with no extended discussion of the historical origin of the tool or how it has been used in particular AI programs. The focus is on techniques abstracted from their historical origins.

The original version of the catalogue, was hastily built in 1983 as part of the UK SERC-DoI, IKBS, Architecture Study [IKBS Architecture Study 83]. It has now been adopted by the SERC Specially Promoted Programme in IKBS and is kept as an on-line document undergoing constant revision and refinement and published as a paperback by Springer Verlag.

The on-line and paperback versions of the catalogue meet different needs and differ in the entries they contain. In particular, the on-line version was designed to promote UK interaction and contains all the entries which we received that meet the criteria defined below. The paperback version was designed to serve as a reference book for the international community, and does not contain entries which are only of interest in a UK context.

By 'AI techniques' we mean algorithms, data (knowledge) formalisms, architectures, and methodological techniques, which can be described in a precise, clean way. The catalogue entries are intended to be non-technical and brief, but with a literature reference. The reference might not be the 'classic' one. It will often be to a textbook or survey article. The border between AI and non-AI techniques is fuzzy. Since the catalogue is to promote interaction some techniques are included because they are vital parts of many AI programs, even though they did not originate in AI.

By 'portable AI software' we mean programming languages, shells, packages, toolkits etc. which are available for use by AI researchers outside the group of the implementor, including both commercial and non-commercial products. To obtain a copy of software, do NOT write to us or the contributor of the entry; look at the 'Availability' field or write to the implementor. We hope that (s)he will supply sufficient documentation for the system to be used by an outsider, but do not expect non-commercial products to be as professionally polished as commercial ones.

In this version of the catalogue we have not included separate entries for each slight variation of a technique, programming language, etc. Neither have we always included details of how to obtain the software, nor descriptions of AI programs tied to a particular application, nor of descriptions of work in progress. The catalogue is not intended to be a dictionary of AI terminology nor to include definitions of AI problems.

Entries are short (abstract length) descriptions of a technique or piece of software. They include a title, list of aliases, contributor's name, paragraph of description, information on availability and references. The contributor's name is that of the original contributor of the entry. Only occasionally is the contributor of the entry also the implementor of the software or the inventor of the technique. The 'Availability' field or the reference are a better guide to the identity of the implementor or inventor. Some entries have been subsequently modified by the referees and/or editorial team, but there has not been time to check these modifications with the original contributor, so (s)he should not always be held morally responsible, and should never be held legally responsible.

Cross references to other entries in the catalogue are marked <N>; where N is the reference number of the entry. The entries are listed and numbered in alphabetic order. There are two indexes to help you find entries: one, the 'Logical Table of Contents', lists the entries under various subfields of AI; and one, the 'Index of Definitions', is a topic/keyword **index**. Both indexes refer to the numbers of the entries rather than the numbers of the pages they occur on. Words that appear in the index are in **boldface** in the text.

Suggestions about the organisation or content of the catalogue are welcomed, and should be sent to:

Alan Bundy,
Department of Artificial Intelligence,
University of Edinburgh,   Tel: (44)-(31)-667-1011 ext 6507
Hope Park Square,
Edinburgh, EH8 9NW,   SERCnet: Bundy@EDXA
Scotland.   ARPAnet: Bundy@Rutgers

                                                        Alan Bundy

<u>References</u>

[IKBS Architecture Study 83]
            Intelligent Knowledge Based Systems: A Programme for Action in the
            UK
            SERC-DoI.   1983.
            Available from Mr W.P. Sharpe, Rutherford Appleton Laboratory,
                Didcot, Oxon, OX11 0QX.

FOREWORD

"Yep, Butcher, nine words. In English it would take a couple of books full of schematics and electrical and architectural specifications. They have the proper nine words. We don't"

Samuel R. Delany
Babel-17

This catalogue has a descriptive and a prescriptive role – it tries to say both what AI is, and what it should be. The descriptive role grew from my beliefs about the nature of AI, and the prescriptive role grew from of my dissatisfaction with the methodology of AI.   In brief my views are as follows.

- There is a methodological malaise in AI, the symptoms of which are: (a) differences among referees and critics as to the criteria for judging AI research, (b) the fragility of AI programs, and (c) the difficulty of rebuilding AI programs from published descriptions.

- This malaise can be cured if AI researchers can agree on the nature of AI, on the methodology for pursuing it and on the criteria for assessing it.

- In order to understand the nature of AI it is necessary to separate off computer science, knowledge engineering and cognitive science from mainstream AI, just as pure maths, engineering and physics are separated off from applied maths.

- That mainstream AI is best viewed as: "the investigation of computational techniques which have the potential of exhibiting intelligent behaviour".

These views are developed more fully in [Bundy 81, Bundy 83a, Bundy 83b].

The core of mainstream AI consists of the techniques which AI has developed to date.   In listing them in this catalogue, I hope we have revealed this core, and thus produced a useful reference work for people in the field.   Of course, that is not all there is to AI.   Firstly, we have not attempted to go into the details of the techniques, nor even to describe them in an algorithmic manner.   We have not described the relations between the techniques, nor their advantages, limitations nor history.   Secondly, experienced researchers share a common set of benchmark problems, a common methodology and a common set of assessment criteria.   We hope that the references we have provided with each technique, will serve as a pointer into the literature which will enable the reader to recover this information.

But thirdly, we have by no means succeeded in an exhaustive coverage of AI techniques.   Part of the blame for this must lie with the editor and review committee for failing to collect all that is available.   Part of the blame, however, lies with the methodological malaise mentioned above; the techniques have just not been distilled from the programs in which they were developed.   The programs have been described in the 'look ma, no hands' style, i.e. the performance of the program has been described with inadequate explanation or discussion of the techniques which enabled this performance.   Even where techniques have been described adequately, the terminological confusion in the field has made it difficult to decide where a new technique is being described with old terminology, and where an old technique is being described with new terminology.

This is where the prescriptive role of the catalogue comes into play. I hope that AI researchers will feel obliged to fit their work into the catalogue, and this will force them to be explicit about the techniques they have invented, improved or tested. I hope that the terminology used in the catalogue will become standard, so that people will stop inventing new terms for old ideas. On the other hand, I hope that the definitions of the old terms in the catalogue will prevent people reusing the old terminology in a new way, and that the authors of the catalogue will be forced to tease apart any different uses of current terms, and rename them. I also hope that researchers will be encouraged to undertake analytic research, investigating the properties of existing techniques, generalizing them, and discovering their interrelations.

In order to play this role it is vital that the catalogue be dynamic, so I am delighted that the SERC have agreed to maintain it as an on-line document, and that Springer Verlag have agreed to reprint it, periodically. Please read through this catalogue with a critical eye, and with the following questions in mind.

- Where would my work fit it here? What techniques have I invented, improved or tested?

- How could this catalogue be improved? Which techniques are missing? Which techniques are poorly explained? Which explanations are faulty or out-of-date?

- How could these techniques be improved? Which ones could be generalized? Which ones could be made more powerful?

- What aspects of AI research are not captured by this catalogue?

If you have suggestions for the improvement of the catalogue then please send them to me.

The views expressed above are entirely my own, and are not necessarily shared by the members of the review committee or contributors to the catalogue. They had their own grounds for thinking that it was worthwhile to devote time and energy to the catalogue. Whatever their grounds, I am grateful for their efforts.

References

[Bundy 81]   Bundy, A.
Some suggested criteria for assessing AI research.
AISB Quarterly (40-41), 1981.

[Bundy 83a]   Bundy, A.
The nature of AI: A reply to Ohlsson.
AISB Quarterly (47), 1983.

[Bundy 83b]   Bundy, A.
                IKBS Architecture Study Paper.
                In *Proceedings of the workshop at Cosener's House, Abingdon, 6-7th
                    January 1983*, pages Appendix A/16-32.   SERC-DoI, 1983.

LOGICAL TABLE OF CONTENTS

Inference and Reasoning

Knowledge Representation

Learning

ACLS: Analogue concept learning system 3
Classification 32
Contradiction backtracing 43
Discrimination learning 58
Discrimination net 59
Finding common paths 70
Focussing 72
Learning from solution paths 118
Postulating intrinsic properties 185
Precondition analysis 186
Protocol analysis 200
Version spaces 256

Logic Programming

Clausal Form 33
HOPE 96
Horn clauses 97
KRC 114
LOGLISP 129
Micro-PROLOG 144
MPROLOG 150
Negation as failure 154
Resolution 212
POPLOG 183
PROLOG 196
T-PROLOG 249

Natural language

Augmented transition network 14
Bottom-up parsing 20
Breadth-first parsing 24
Cascaded augmented transition network 27
Case frames 28
Chart parsing 30
Conceptual dependency 36
Context-free grammar 41
Definite clause grammar 49
Depth-first parsing 54
Deterministic parsing 56
Discrimination net 59
Earley's Algorithm 64
Functional grammar 80
Generative Capacity 85
Island parsing 109
KRL: knowledge representation language 115
LIFER 120
Meta-rules 141
Partitioned semantic net 172
Plan recognition 179
Predictive parsing 187
Preference semantics 190

Pattern Recognition and Image Processing

Planning

Problem Solving

Vision

1. 2 1/2-D SKETCH

A viewer-centred representation making explicit the depths, local orientations and discontinuities of visible surfaces, created and maintained from a number of cues e.g. **stereopsis** <241> and **optical flow** <167>.   It was thought by Marr to be at the limit of pure perception, i.e. subsequent processes are no longer completely data-driven, and for him it provides a representation of objective physical reality that precedes the decomposition of the scene into objects.

Contributors: T P Pridmore, S R Pollard, S P Stenton.

Reference

[Marr 82]   Marr, D.
              Vision.
              Freeman, 1982.

2. A* ALGORITHM

A form of **heuristic search** <92> that tries to find the cheapest path from the initial state to the goal. Its characteristic feature is the **evaluation function**. This is the sum of two components: the estimated minimum cost of a path from the initial state to the current state, and the estimated cost from the current state to the goal. The first component can be calculated if the **search space** is a tree, or it can be approximated by the cheapest known path if the search space is a graph. The second component must be defined, like any evaluation function, with respect to the domain.   The heuristic power of this method depends on the properties of the evaluation function.

Contributor: Maarten van Someren.

Reference

[Hart, Nilsson and Raphael 68]
              Hart P.E., Nilsson N.J. and Raphael B.
              A formal basis for the heuristic determination of minimum cost
                  paths.
              IEEE Transactions on SSC 4:100-107, 1968.
              A correction was published in SIGART Newsletter 37:28-29,1972.

3. ACLS: ANALOGUE CONCEPT LEARNING SYSTEM

ACLS interactively derives a classification rule in the form of a decision tree, branching according to the values of attribute chosen by an expert to be representative of the problem to be solved.   ACLS can output the rule either as a decision tree or as a Pascal procedure.   ACLS is written in standard Pascal and runs on micros (under UCSD Pascal), minis and main frames.

An enhanced version called EXPERT-EASE for the IBM pc is marketed by Export Software International (Edinburgh).   EXPERT-EASE is a spreadsheet-based, menu-driven package aimed at business and non-technical users.

2

Contributors: Alen Shapiro and A. Paterson.

Availability

Commercially available with documentation and support.

Environment: UCSD Pascal, VAX/VMS Pascal, Berkeley Pascal

From: Donald Michie,   (ACLS)
      Intelligent Terminals Ltd.
      George House, George Square,
      Glasgow,
      Scotland.

Or: Ian Ritchie,   (EXPERT-EASE)
      Export Software International,
      4 Canongate Venture,
      New Street, Royal Mile,
      Edinburgh, EH8 9BH.

4. ACTORS

The actor model of computation was developed by Hewitt (1977) in order to explore the fundamental issues involved with computation via **message-passing**. Actors are objects which know about other actors and can receive messages from other actors.   Each actor is specified by detailing what kind of messages it will receive, and the sequence of actions of the actor, should it be sent one of these messages.   Everything in an actor based programming system is an actor.   To increment a value, for instance, a message would be sent to the actor representing the number, asking the actor to increment itself.   The essential difference between the actor model of computation and the **SmallTalk-80 <236>** language is that the sequencing of computations by actors depends critically on the concept of a "continuation".   A continuation is an actor which is prepared to accept an (intermediate) value as a message, and continue the computation.   In SmallTalk-80, an object (or actor) will instead return a message to the object which instigated the computation, in much the same way that a Pascal function will return a value to the routine which called it.

Contributor: Mark Drummond.

Reference

[Hewitt 77]   Hewitt, C.
                Viewing Control Structures as Patterns of Passing Messages.
                Artificial Intelligence 8:323-364, 1977.

5. AGE

A tool for helping knowledge engineers design, build and test different frameworks for **expert systems**, implemented in **INTERLISP <103>**. Provides an environment in which different representational and control techniques can be explored and developed.   AGE provides the user with two types of entities: components and frameworks; a component is a collection of routines that support basic AI mechanisms e.g. **production rules** <192> and a framework is a predefined configuration of components e.g. **backward chaining, blackboard** <19> AGE contains useful interfaces for building, debugging and explanation, plus **history-recording** facilities.

Contributor: Luis Jenkins.

Availability

Available as a research tool with documentation. Graphic interface is available for the XEROX 1100 systems.

Environment: DEC 20/TOPS, DEC 10/TENEX, XEROX 1100 series.
VAX-Interlisp version under development

From: Juanita Mullen,
Heuristic Programming Project,
Stanford Computer Science Dept.,
Stanford,
CA 94305.

Tel: (415) 497-0474
Electronic address: Mullen@Sumex

References

[Nii]   Nii, H. P.
                          An Introduction to Knowledge Engineering, Blackboard Model, and
                               AGE.
                          Project Report HPP-80-29, Computer Science Dept., Stanford
                               University,

[Nii and Aiello 79]
                          Nii, H. P. and Aiello, N.
                          AGE (Attempt to Generalize): A Knowledge-Based Program for
                               Building Knowledge-Based Programs.
                          In *Proceedings of IJCAI-79*, pages 645-655. International Joint
                               Conference on Artificial Intelligence, 1979.

6. ALICE

Alias: **A**pplicative **L**anguage **I**dealised **C**omputing **E**ngine.

A parallel **graph reduction** machine being designed and built at Imperial College. ALICE is aimed at the efficient execution of declarative languages such as **PROLOG** <196>, and pure LISP <34> although it will support other more conventional languages. The ALICE architecture consists of many processing 'agents' connected to many memory segments through a multi-stage **delta network** and circulating rings connecting the agents to distribute work and free storage locations.

Contributor: John Darlington.

Reference

[Darlington and Reeve 81]
        Darlington, J. and Reeve, M.J.
        ALICE: a multi-processor reduction machine for the efficient
          evaluation of applicative languages.
        In *Proc. MIT/ACM Conference on Functional Languages and Computer
          Architecture*, pages 65-75. 1981.

7. ALPHA/BETA PRUNING

A refinement of **minimax** <145> to determine the optimal move in a game. Nodes that are not needed to evaluate the possible moves of the top node are 'pruned'. Suppose that MAX is to move at parent node P, and that it is known from previous calculations that daughter D1 guarantees a minimum gain of say +20 for MAX. Now we start exploring D2 and discover that the opponent can force a maximal gain of +10 by reacting to D2 with D2.1. In this case there is no need to explore other daughters of D2, because MAX can never gain more than +10 and therefore will always prefer D1. Following this line of reasoning, both from the point of view of MAX and of MIN, large parts of the tree need not be explored and an optimal solution will still be found.

Contributor: Maarten van Someren.

Reference

(Barr and Feigenbaum 81)
        Barr, A. and Feigenbaum, E.A. (editors).
        The Handbook of Artificial Intelligence Vol.1.
        Kaufmann, 1981.

8. AL/X

AL/X is an **expert system** shell developed by the University of Edinburgh and Intelligent Terminals Limited. It was originally developed to assist in the diagnosis of underlying causes of automatic shutdowns on oil production platforms. AL/X has been used by several industrial companies to evaluate expert systems.

It is a **backward chaining**, probabilistic system, and is similar to the **Prospector** inference engine.

Contributor: Martin Merry.

Availability

Commercially available with documentation.

Environment: Standard Pascal, UCSD Pascal, VAX-VMS Pascal, Berkeley Pascal
                (Also most micros)

From: Donald Michie,

Intelligent Terminals Ltd.
George House, George Square,
Glasgow,
Scotland.

Reference

[Reiter 80]   Reiter, J.
                AL/X: An Expert System using Plausible Inference.
                Technical Report, Intelligent Terminals Limited, June, 1980.

9. AMORD

AMORD is a deductive procedure system based on a non-chronological control structure and a system of automatically maintained data **dependencies**.   AMORD is intended to be used for writing problem solvers.   One of its principal features is the way it encourages the use of explicit control of reasoning.   The data dependencies are maintained in AMORD by the use of a **truth maintenance system <250>**.   A **MACLISP <132>** interpreter for AMORD can be found in [de Kleer et al 78].

Contributor: Kevin Poulter.

Reference

[de Kleer et al 78]
                de Kleer, J., et al.
                AMORD: A Deductive Procedure System.
                AI Memo 435, MIT, January, 1978.

10. ANALOGICAL PROBLEM SOLVING

A technique whereby the current problem is solved by retrieving from memory a previously solved similar problem and appropriately adapting that problem's solution.

Carbonell (1981) has developed a particular version of this technique based on **means/ends analysis <138>**.

Contributor: Jim Doran.

Reference

[Carbonell 81]   Carbonell, Jaime G.
                A Computational Model of Analogical Problem Solving.
                In Proceedings of IJCAI-81.   IJCAI, 1981.

11. APES

A **PROLOG <196> expert system** shell currently implemented in **Micro-PROLOG <144>**.   Knowledge bases are defined as sets of PROLOG **clauses**.

Contributors: Peter Hammond and Mark Sergot.

Availability

Commercially available with documentation. Available to academic institutions on request.

Environment: 8086/88 with MSDOS/CPM86, Unix

From: Peter Hammond,
      Department of Computing,
      Imperial College,
      180 Queens Gate,
      London SW7 2BZ.

      Tel: 01-589-5111 Ext 2771

References

[Hammond 82] Hammond, P.
              The APES System: A user manual.
              Research Report 82/9, Department of Computing, Imperial College,
              1982.

[Hammond & Sergot 83]
              Hammond, P. and Sergot, M.J.
              A PROLOG Shell for Logic Based Expert Systems.
              In *Proceedings of BCS Expert Systems '83*. BCS Expert Systems,
              Cambridge, 1983.

12. ARBY

ARBY is an expert system shell, written in **FranzLisp**, intended for diagnostic applications. Current applications of ARBY include fault isolation systems for avionics Automatic Test Equipment (ATE) and a distributed inventory network.

ARBY is based on a predicate calculus notation and uses the **DUCK** deductive system, a set of LISP routines which implement a **relational database** similar to those found in **Prolog <196>** and **PLANNER <143>**.

Contributor: Kevin Poulter.

Availability

Commercially available with documentation and informal support.

Environment: VAX 11/780 under VMS, APOLLO running T (forthcoming) and
            Symbolics 3600 running ZetaLisp (forthcoming).
            ARBY requires the DUCK deductive system.

From: Eamon Barrett,
      Smart Systems Technology,
      Suite 300, 6870 Elm street,

McLean, VA 22101,
USA.

Tel: (703) 448-8562

Reference

[McDermott and Brooks 82]
McDermott, D., and Brooks, R.
ARBY: Diagnosis with Shallow Causal Models.
In *AAAI-82*. AAAI, 1982.

13. ASSOCIATIVE DATABASE

Associative database with **pattern directed retrieval** by the "Get Possibilities/Try Next" mechanism. Provision of **context** layers as in **CONNIVER** <38> and **QA4** <203> allows for items to be associated with a value in some particular context.

Contributor: Austin Tate.

14. AUGMENTED TRANSITION NETWORK

Alias: **ATN**.

Representation for grammars developed from simple **finite state transition networks** by allowing (a) recursion and (b) augmentation, i.e. the use of arbitrary tests and actions on arcs, giving full Turing machine power. The use of registers for storing constituents, and the use of tests and actions on register contents allow great flexibility in parsing, and in particular permit the construction of sentence representations quite distinct from the surface text e.g. deep as opposed to surface syntactic structures. The form of grammar representation is procedurally oriented, but the grammar itself is separated from the interpretive parser, which is **top-down** <248> and usually **depth-first** <55>. ATNs are a popular formalism and can be adapted e.g. to guide parsing by explicit arc ordering. Problems arise with e.g. passing information between subnets, and the treatment of conjunctions.

Contributor: Karen Sparck Jones.

Reference

[Woods 70]   Woods, W.A.
Transition network grammars for natural language analysis.
Communications of the ACM 13:591-606, 1970.

15. B* ALGORITHM

Alias: **alpha/beta pruning**.

B* is a **heuristic search** method that can be applied to both adversary and non-adversary problems, but only when the search has an iterative character. It computes the best next step toward the solution on the basis of an evaluation function.

An evaluation function assigns two values to each node, a pessimistic and an optimistic value, (c.f. **minimax** <145>) on the basis of evaluation of the descendants. In non-adversary search this is done according to the following rules:

1. Evaluate the descendants of a node in arbitrary order. If one of the descendants of a node has a pessimistic value greater than the pessimistic value of its parent, then raise the pessimistic value of the parent to the value of this daughter. If a node has an optimistic value that is higher than that of any daughter, than lower it to the maximal optimistic value of its daughters.

2. Terminate when a daughter of the root of the search tree has a pessimistic value that is not lower than the optimistic value of all other daughters. The arc to that daughter is the best step to do.

In the case of adversary search (game playing), B* is the same as **alpha/beta search** <7>, except that it stops once it has found the best next move. **Heuristic** or **best first search** <92> may be implemented in this manner. B* is claimed to be a good model of the search of chess masters.

Contributor: Maarten van Someren.

Reference

[Berliner 79]   Berliner, H.
The B* tree search algorithm: a best-first proof procedure.
Artificial Intelligence 12: 23–40, 1979.

16. BANDPASS FILTER

Bandpass filter is one which allows a band of spatial frequencies to pass through it. This band can be described in terms of the value of its peak frequency and its width at half amplitude. See **spatial frequency channels** <238>.

Contributors: T P Pridmore, S R Pollard, S T Stenton.

Reference

[Campbell]   Campbell, F.W.C.
Sometimes a Biologist has to Make a Noise Like A Mathematician.
Prog. Bull. 15: 417–424.

17. BAYESIAN INFERENCE

Alias: **statistical inference**.

Bayesian inference is one means by which knowledge based systems can reason when uncertainty is involved.   Given an hypothesis event H and an evidence event E, we obtain from an expert estimates of the prior probabilities P(H) and P(E), and the conditional probability P(E/H).   From Bayes' Rule we obtain the probability of H given evidence E. This is calculated as:

$$P(H/E) = \frac{P(E/H) \cdot P(H)}{P(E)}$$

In practical problems E may be any subset of the set of all possible evidence events and H may be any subset of the set of all possible hypotheses.   This tends to require a vast number of conditional probabilities to be calculated.

An alternative approach is therefore to combine with a **rule based system <192>** where conditional probabilities are given only for each rule.   This approach is adequate until we consider the **local updating problem** which arises when two or more inference rules make a conclusion about the same hypothesis.   This problem has only been solved by various ad hoc means.

An example of the use of Bayesian inference is the **Prospector** system.

Contributor: Robert Corlett.

Reference

[Duda, Hart and Nilsson 76]
Duda, R., Hart, P., and Nilsson, N.
Subjective Bayesian Methods for Rule-Based Inference Systems.
In *AFIPS Conference Proceedings*.   AFIPS, 1976.

18. BIDIRECTIONAL SEARCH

In bidirectional search of a **state space <240>**, search proceeds both backwards and forwards.   The program terminates when a common state is reached, since this means that a path has been found from the initial state to the goal state.

Contributor: Maarten van Someren.

Reference

(Barr and Feigenbaum 81)
Barr, A. and Feigenbaum, E.A. (editors).
The Handbook of Artificial Intelligence Vol. 1.
Kaufmann, 1981.

19. BLACKBOARD

An architectural technique developed principally for continuous reasoning 'real-time' systems. Based on the concept of 'experts' sitting round a blackboard it attempts to co-ordinate the activities of a number of different **Knowledge Sources** (KS) by providing a global database between them, to which partial solutions to the problem under examination are posted.

The Blackboard is divided into a number of abstraction levels, each one containing hypotheses for partial solutions linked to other levels by logical relationships; a Monitor controls access to these hypotheses and inspects any changes in order to notify KSs of those of interest.

Each KS is independent of all others and interfaces externally in a uniform way that is identical across KSs and in which no KS knows which or how many others exist. In general, a KS monitors a level of the Blackboard for conditions for which its knowledge is applicable, it then proposes to process those conditions by placing an item on the **agenda**. The agenda is a list of possible processing events from which the **scheduler** must choose the one most likely to lead to a complete problem solution. This decision making process can be controlled by a static set of rules about problem solving and a dynamic goal structure, which change as the solution progresses, to focus attention in a data-directed fashion. The chosen event is passed for execution to its instantiating KS.

The Blackboard idea has also been extended to a hierarchical model, with differing concepts on different blackboards and knowledge sources 'piping' information between blackboards in the form of expectations, supports, refutations, etc.

Contributors: Martin Bennet, John Lumley.

References

[Erman and Lesser 75]
> Erman, L.D. and Lesser, V.R.
> A Multi-Level Organisation for Problem Solving Using Many, Diverse, Cooperating Sources of Knowledge.
> In *Proceedings of IJCAI-75*, pages 483-490. International Joint Conference on Artificial Intelligence, 1975.

[Erman et al 80]
> Erman, L.D., Hayes-Roth, F., Lesser, V.R., and Reddy, D.R.
> The Hearsay II Speech Understanding System: Integrating Knowledge to Resolve Uncertainty.
> *Computing Surveys* 12(2), June, 1980.

20. BOTTOM-UP PARSING

Alias: **data-driven parsing**.

In trying to parse a string with a grammar, if one starts with the string and tries to fit it to the grammar, this is **bottom-up** or **data-driven** parsing. For instance with a **context-free grammar** <41>, one starts with a token in the string and works up from there on the basis of rules in the grammar which have that token on their right hand side, trying to reduce eventually to the initial symbol.

Contributor: Henry Thompson.

Reference

[Winograd 83]   Winograd, T.
                 Language as a cognitive process.
                 Addison-Wesley, 1983.

21. BOUNDARY DETECTION

Alias: **line finding, curve detection**.

The conventional approach to **image segmentation <99>** in early visual processing is **edge detection <65>** followed by boundary detection.   Edge detection produces primitive edge elements, possibly with properties of magnitude and/or direction, at places in the image where the edge detection operator has "fired".   The task of the boundary detection process is to produce a set of boundaries by appropriately connecting up primitive edge elements.   There are two main methods:

- **boundary tracking**

- the **generalised Hough transform <84>**

Since a boundary is, by definition, a connected set of edge elements, the obvious approach is to choose any edge element and look for its neighbours, which are then connected to the initial element to form a boundary.   This search process is then continually repeated for the elements at the ends of the boundary until some termination criterion is met (such as not being able to find any nearby neighbours). In the Hough transform technique, each primitive edge element is transformed into a curve in a transform space representing all the possible boundaries the edge element could be part of.   The **transform-space** curves produced by edge elements on the same image boundary should all intersect at the same point in transform space, which can be subjected to the inverse transform to characterise the boundary in the image.   Originally applicable to straight boundaries only, this method has been generalised to deal with any curve describable in an analytic or tabular form.

Contributor: Bob Beattie.

Reference

[Ballard and Brown 82]
                 Ballard, D.H. and Brown, C.M.
                 Computer Vision.
                 Prentice-Hall Inc., 1982, chapter 5.

22. BOYER-MOORE THEOREM PROVER

This is an **automatic theorem proving** program, whose underlying formalism is **recursive function theory**. The system is designed to prove theorems by continuous application of **rewrite rules** <213> and **structural induction**. The key feature of the program is the heuristics it uses to guide the search. In particular, there are powerful heuristics for the automatic use of induction. Some guidance by the user is necessary, by specifying which lemmas must be known before the goal theorem is attempted. Lemmas must be proved by the system before they are automatically used, so the theorem prover is assured of the validity of the proof of the final theorem. The system is not complete, however, since some heuristics generalise the theorem. Its standard set consists of 400 theorems, including the soundness and completeness of a tautology checker for propositional calculus, the equivalence of interpreted and optimized compiled code for a simple arithmetic language, the correctness of a fast string-searching algorithm, the prime-factorization theorem and the unsolvability of the halting problem.

Contributor: Leon Sterling.

Reference

[Boyer and Moore 79]
Boyer R., Moore J.
ACM Monograph: A Computational Logic.
Academic Press, 1979.

23. BRANCH-AND-BOUND ALGORITHMS

A solution technique for **discrete optimisation** problems which is widely used outside AI and is closely related to the **A* algorithm** <2>. The task is to find the optimally valued tip of a walkable search tree. A subtree of the search tree need not be searched if a computation at its root yields a bound for its set of tip values which implies that none of them can be optimal.

Contributor: Jim Doran.

Reference

[Aho Hopcroft and Ullman 83]
Aho A.V., Hopcroft J.E. and Ullman J.D.
Data Structures and Algorithms.
Addison-Wesley, 1983, pages 330-336.

24. BREADTH-FIRST PARSING

Amounts to **breadth-first searching** <25> of the tree of alternatives which arise in the parsing process. The opposite of **depth-first parsing** <54>.

Contributor: Henry Thompson.

Reference

[Winograd 83]   Winograd, T.
                 Language as a cognitive process.
                 Addison-Wesley, 1983.

25. BREADTH-FIRST SEARCH

An uninformed **graph searching** strategy in which each level is searched before going to the next deeper level.   This strategy guarantees finding the shortest path to the node sought first: any path to the solution that is of length n will be found when the search reaches depth n, and this is guaranteed to be before any node of depth > n is searched.

Contributor: Dave Plummer.

Reference

[Nilsson 82]   Nilsson, N.J.
                 Principles of Artificial Intelligence.
                 Tioga Pub. Co., 1982.

26. CAMBRIDGE LISP

An implementation of **LISP** similar in dialect to Standard LISP.   Written in a high level language it was originally designed for IBM System 360 architecture, but is also available for MC68000 and GEC System 63.   The HLH Orion implementation is being prepared as are other implementations.   Cambridge LISP is a production quality LISP, incorporating many checking facilities for safe code without impacting efficiency.   For example car/cdr checking are available in compiled code, and the interpreter maintains additional information to provide a great deal of security.

The compiler is a variation of the Hearn/Griss portable compiler, and the editor is based on the UCI editor.

The language contains syntax extension via read macros, vectors, rational infinite precision numbers, strings, floating point numbers as well as list structure and binary programs.

The origin of Cambridge LISP is in symbolic mathematics, hence its richness of numeric types, but it has been extensively used for AI and natural language.   A slow PROLOG <196> is available under Cambridge LISP.

Contributor: John Fitch.

Availability

Commercially available with documentation and support.

Environment: BCPL compiler, with extentions.

From: Prof. John Fitch,
      School of Mathematics,
      University of Bath,
      Claverton Down,
      Bath BA2 7AY.

      Tel: (0225) 61244 Ext 820
      Electronic address: fitch@ucl-cs, fitch@utah-20, jpfl@camphx

Or: GEC COMPUTERS (for SYSTEM 63)

Or: Sirius Microtech Ltd. (for Dark Star)
    Malvern Link,
    Worcester.

References

[Fitch and Norman 77]
                J.P. Fitch and A.C. Norman.
                Implementing LISP in a High Level Language.
                Software - Practice and Experience , 1977.

[Fitch and Norman 83]
                J.P. Fitch and A.C. Norman.
                Cambridge LISP Manual.
                Technical Report, University of Bath, 1983.

27. CASCADED AUGMENTED TRANSITION NETWORK

   Alias: **CATN**.

Extension of **augmented transition network <14>** parsing to use a sequence of ordinary ATNs that include among the actions on their arcs a special operation to transmit an element to the next ATN 'machine' in the sequence, with the first machine in the **cascade** taking its input from the input string.   Provides a framework for separating e.g. syntactic, semantic and discourse tracking specifications into a cascade of ATNs, one (or more) for each domain.   This clean separation of levels of processing means that different higher level partial hypotheses can share the same lower level processing, which in turn can be more flexible due to the loose coupling between the ATN machines (c.f.   coupling between subnetworks in an ordinary ATN).

   Contributor: Henry Thompson.

Reference

[Woods 80]   Woods, W.A.
               Cascaded ATN Grammars.
               American Journal of Computational Linguistics 6:1-12, 1980.

28. CASE FRAMES

A widely used device for the determination and representation of text meaning, based on the organisation of information primarily round verbs, or actions, by **case roles**, e.g. **Agent**, **Instrument**, **Location**. Case frames are ordinarily micro-structures oriented towards linguistic units like sentences, as opposed to the knowledge-oriented macro-structures of **frames** <77>. Though reference to Fillmore's linguistically-motivated ideas is conventional, there is great variation in the treatment of every aspect of case frames, e.g. their relation to features of the **surface text** (is the sentence subject the Agent?), their number (ten or thirty?), their status (obligatory or optional?), the constraints on their fillers (is the Agent HUMAN?), etc. **Conceptual dependency <36>**, for example, uses a small number of deep cases.

Contributor: Karen Sparck Jones.

Reference

[Bruce 75]   Bruce, B.
Case systems for natural language.
Artificial Intelligence 6:327-360, 1975.

29. CELLULAR ARRAYS

A class of parallel computers consisting of an array of small processors each executing the same instruction on its local data. The processors are often one bit processors (a bit-serial array) and are often arranged in a regular lattice using hexagonal or square tessellation (with or without diagonals). Such arrays are particularly useful for simple image processing where each **image pixel** is generally assigned to a separate processor (eg. [Danielsson 1981]). Typical examples are **DAP** (from ICL), **CLIP4** (from University College London), **MPP** (from Goodyear Aerospace) and **GRID** (from GEC). See **propagation in cellular arrays <197>**.

Contributor: Dave Reynolds.

Reference

[Danielsson and Levialdi 81]
Danielsson P-E. and Levialdi S.
Computer Architectures for Pictorial Information Systems.
Computer 14(11):53-67, November, 1981.

30. CHART PARSING

Chart parsing is an approach to **non-deterministic parsing** developed by Kay and Kaplan based on earlier work by Earley, Kay and Colmerauer. In contrast to that earlier work, in which the **chart** was a (in some cases enriched) **well-formed substring table** for recording intermediate results, the later systems use the chart as the active agent in the parsing process.

The chart is a directed graph, with two sorts of edges - active and inactive. Inactive edges record the existence of complete constituents.   Active edges record hypothesised incomplete constituents. The parsing process itself consists of adding new edges in response to the meeting of active with inactive edges. As a record of an incomplete constituent, an active edge must carry some indication of how it may be extended, e.g. a dotted **context-free rule** or a state in a **network grammar** (**RTN** or **ATN** <14>). When an **active edge** and an **inactive edge** meet for the first time, if the inactive edge satisfies the active edge's conditions for extension, then a new edge will be constructed.

If initial hypotheses about constituents are keyed by active edges and their needs, parsing will be **top-down** <248>. If on the other hand these hypotheses are keyed by inactive edges, parsing will be **bottom-up** <20>. One of the principal advantages of the chart parsing methodology is that it easily supports a variety of grammatical formalisms, rule invocation strategies, and control regimes. See (Thompson and Ritchie 1983) for an elementary introduction, and (Kay 1980) for a detailed theoretical analysis.

Contributor: Henry Thompson.

References

[Kay 80]   Kay, M.
                Algorithm Schemata and Data Structures in Syntactic Processing.
                In *Proceedings of the Nobel Symposium on Text Processing*. Nobel
                    Academy, 1980.
                Also available as CSL-80-12, Xerox PARC, Palo Alto, CA.

[Thompson and Ritchie 83]
                Thompson, H.S. and Ritchie, G.D.
                Techniques for Parsing Natural Language: Two Examples.
                In Eisenstadt and O'Shea (editors), *Artificial Intelligence Skills*.
                    Harper and Row, 1983.
                Also available as Research Paper 183, Department of Artificial
                    Intelligence, University of Edinburgh.

31. CHI

CHI is an integrated environment of knowledge-based tools <201> that assist with various aspects of the process of building computing systems. These tools include: a very-high-level, wide spectrum language named **V** used to express not only software specifications but also programming knowledge; a program transformation component and a set of rules (in V) for **program synthesis**, including data structure generation; a constraint maintenance system; and a program/knowledge editor and debugger. Designed but not yet fully implemented for the CHI system are: support for project management and integrated communication facilities for documentation, bug reports, message sending, etc.

Contributor: Cordell Green.

References

[Green and Westfold 82]
        Green, C. and Westfold, S.
        Knowledge-Based Programming Self-Applied.
        In Hayes, P., Michie, D. and Pac, Y-H. (editors), *Machine Intelligence 10*, . Ellis Horwood Ltd, Halsted Press, 1982.
        Also available as Technical Report KES. U. 81. 4, Kestrel Institute, Palo Alto, CA, March 1981.

[Kedzierski 82]   Kedzierski, B.
        Communication and Management Support in System Development Environments.
        Technical Report KES. U. 82. 3, Kestrel Institute, 1982.
        Also appeared in Proceedings of the Conference on Human Factors in Computer Systems, Gaithersburg, Maryland, March 1982.

[Phillips 83]   Phillips, J.
        Self-Described Programming Environments: An Application of a Theory of Design to Programming Systems.
        PhD thesis, Stanford University, 1983.
        Also available as Technical Report KES. U. 83. 1, Kestrel Institute, Palo Alto, CA, February 1983.

32. CLASSIFICATION

Alias: **ID3**.

A **discrimination net** <59> can be built from a set of classified items. The set is repeatedly split into subsets by the value of a predicate, until each subset contains members of one class only. The series of splits defines the **discrimination net**.

To increase the efficiency of the resulting discrimination net, the predicates on which the items are split are chosen using information theoretic techniques so that they make the number of instances in each subset as similar as possible. This technique has been successfully applied to the problem of classifying chess positions as won or drawn.

Contributor: Maarten Van Someren.

Reference

[Quinlan 79]   Quinlan, J. R.
        Discovering rules by induction from large collections of examples.
        In Michie, D. (editor), *Expert systems in the Micro-electronic Age*. Edinburgh University Press, 1979.

33. CLAUSAL FORM

A normal form for **predicate calculus** <189> formulae borrowed from **mathematical logic**, and much used in **automatic theorem proving**. It consists of applying **prenex normal form**, **Skolemization** <235> and **conjunctive normal form**, in succession. The resulting formula has a model if and only if the original formula does. A formula in clausal form consists of a conjunction of clauses. Each **clause** is a disjunction of literals. Each **literal** is either an **atomic sentence** or the negation of an atomic sentence, where an atomic sentence is a predicate applied to some terms.

Contributor: Alan Bundy.

Reference

[Chang and Lee 73]
Chang, C. and Lee, R. C.
Symbolic Logic and Mechanical Theorem Proving.
Academic Press, 1973.

34. COMMON LISP

"The foremost aim of the Common LISP project is not to completely standardize LISP, nor is it necessarily to design the most beautiful possible LISP. It is to agree on a common subset that can be supported efficiently in a wide variety of hardware and software environments and within which large amounts of software can be written and shared among several implementations." Common LISP provides most of the facilities provided by any 'modern' LISP (eg. **MACLISP** <132>, **INTERLISP** <103>). In addition, Common LISP provides fully lexically scoped variables, a rich set of numerical data types, strings, arrays and vectors, bit and field manipulation, non-local exits and user controlable error handling, a hash facility, user-defined data types (Defstruct), stream-based I/O, and formatting and pretty-printing facilities. Common LISP does not provide graphics primitives, multiprocessing, or object-oriented programming; however, it is expected that any given implementation will provide a superset of Common LISP which may provide these facilities. Common LISP is expected to evolve to include some of these facilities as they become more standardized. Several implementations of Common LISP are under way; a few of these are nearing completion.

Contributor: Joseph Ginder.

Reference

[Steele et al. 82]
Steele, G. L. Jr. et al.
An Overview of Common LISP.
In *Proceedings of the 1982 ACM Symposium on Lisp and Functional Programming*, pages 98-170. ACM, 1982.

35. COMPUTER AUDIOMETRY

Alias: Speech & Hearing.

This technique provides a means for plotting an **audiogram** (given a graphics capability). The algorithm evaluates a person's threshold of hearing by playing a sequence of tones at various frequencies and amplitudes (using a programmable tone generator). The person simply has to answer "yes" or "no" with one of two push buttons, as to whether or not he/she can hear the tone; the amplitude decreases until he just can not hear it, otherwise the amplitude increases until he just can hear it. A range of frequencies is tested by playing the tones in ascending octaves, and then in descending octaves and averaging out the results. The audiogram is then plotted on a graphics terminal.

Contributor: Peter Mitchell.

36. CONCEPTUAL DEPENDENCY

Theory of meaning representation developed by Schank and extensively exploited at Yale, relying on deep 'conceptual' **semantic primitives <228>** and **case frames <28>** and providing a strong decomposition of word and text meaning. The emphasis on key **primitive acts** and required properties of the fillers of their (obligatory) roles is used to drive primarily **semantic expectation-based parsing**.

Contributor: Karen Sparck Jones.

Reference

[Schank 75]   Schank, R.C. (editor).
                Conceptual Information Processing.
                North-Holland, 1975.

37. CONNECTION MACHINE

The connection machine is a special architecture being developed at MIT for concurrently manipulating knowledge stored in **semantic networks <227>**. The connection machine avoids the problems of manipulating semantic nets on a sequential machine by giving each node and link in the network its own simple processor.

The connection machine is not intended for use as a general-purpose parallel computer, but to be very fast at a few simple operations that are important for Artificial Intelligence applications (e.g. searching, deduction from semantic inheritance networks).

Contributor: Kevin Poulter.

Reference

[Hillis 81]   Hillis, W.D.
                The Connection Machine.
                AI Memo 646, MIT, September, 1981.

38. CONNIVER

CONNIVER was developed by Sussman and McDermott in response to the shortcomings of **PLANNER <143>**. It is implemented in **MACLISP <132>**. CONNIVER provides various control primitives to allow the programmer to specify more flexible control regimes. Perhaps the most important contributions of CONNIVER are the **context** and **coroutining** primitives that it provides.

CONNIVER supports all the PLANNER data structures and in addition provides the user with context tags and **possibility lists**. The **consequent** and **antecedent** theorems of PLANNER become the **if-needed**, **if-added**, and **if-removed** methods of CONNIVER. All the solutions to a given goal may be collected and stored on a possibility list. Coroutining facilities allow the suspension and activation of processes, enabling the programmer to specify other than a **depth-first search** <55> of the **search space**.

The CONNIVER database is organised into contexts. Assertions and methods (theorems) are true in a certain context which may be created from other existing contexts and moved to by use of the "tag" or name associated with each context. The context mechanisms allows flexibility in the order of solution of subgoals; work on one subgoal may be suspended while another is solved, attention returning to the original subgoal (whose state has been saved) at a later date.

Contributor: Lincoln Wallen.

Reference

[Sussman and McDermott 72]
        Sussman, G. J. and McDermott, D. V.
        From PLANNER to CONNIVER: A genetic approach.
        In *AFIPS*, pages 1171-1180. 1972.

39. CONSTRAINT SATISFACTION AND PROPAGATION

Alias: **consistent-labeling**, **satisfaction assignment**.

Many problems in Artificial Intelligence, Operations Research and Symbolic Logic can be seen as special cases of this general **NP-complete** problem; for example, some problems that are naturally viewed in this way are **scene labeling** and **scene matching** or more generally, the relational homomorphism problem, finding spanning trees and Euler tours in a graph, space planning problems, data-base **consistency-maintenance**, **query-answering** and **redundancy-checking** and many puzzles such as **cryptarithmetic**. Other examples are: the Boolean Satisfiability problems, Graph and Sub-graph Isomorphism detection, the graph coloring problem, packing problems, finding Hamiltonian circuits in a graph and **edge detection** <65> in a scene.

The **Constraint-Satisfaction Problem** consists of a finite set $V = \{ v_1 \ldots v_n \}$ of n **variables**. The i-th variable v_i has an associated finite domain $D_i = \{ v_{i1} \ldots v_{iM} \}$ from which it can take any of M_i **values** or **labels** (not necessarily numerical). A **set** $R = \{ R_1 \ldots R_m \}$ of **constraint relations** is given specifying which values are mutually compatible for various subsets of the n variables. In particular the j-th constraint

$$R_j \leq D_{ij_1} \times D_{ij_2} \times \ldots \times D_{ij_{r_j}}$$

specifies which tuples of values are consistent labelings for its r_j argument variables, ij_k being the k-th argument. Note that the constraints R_j may in practice be given either as truth-tables, or as lists of only the satisfying tuples or, more concisely, in analytic form as expressions (such as $v_3^2 + v_5 \leq 9$) in some "constraint languages", algebraic or otherwise. The **goal** is to find all solution-tuples from $D_1 \times \ldots \times D_n$, i.e those in which the n assignments of values to variables satisfy all problem constraints simultaneously. See also the entry on **relaxation labelling** <210>.

A technique for propagating constraints on variables throughout a symbolic plan has been developed by Stefik in the **MOLGEN** program. During the planning stage a **top-down** series of decisions, notably variable instantiations, must be made. Each decision may well have implications at a point in the plan other than that at which it was made. In this context, constraint propagation is a process by which constraints on variables imposed by such decisions are passed via **explicit** operators to take effect elsewhere in the plan structure.

Contributors: Jim Doran and B.A. Nudel.

References

[Nudel 83]   Nudel, B.A.
                Consistent-labeling problems and their algorithms: expected-
                    complexities and theory-based heuristics.
                Artificial Intelligence 20, 1983.
                Special issue on Search and Heuristics, in memory of John
                    Gaschnig; to appear.

[Stefik 80]   Stefik, M.J.
                Planning with constraints (Molgen: part 1).
                Artificial Intelligence 14, 1980.

[Waltz 75]   Waltz, D.L.
                Understanding line drawings of scenes with shadows.
                In Winston, P.H. (editor), *The Psychology of Computer Vision*.
                    McGraw-Hill, New York, 1975.

40. CONSTRUCTIVE SOLID GEOMETRY

A method of constructing **solid models** in which a set of primitive solids is provided (e.g. cuboids, cylinders), and further solids are created by either moving a solid in space, or by set combinations of solids (i.e. set union, intersection, or difference). The technique has been put on a firm theoretical basis [Requicha and Voelker 80].

Spatial Decomposition: A technique applicable to **geometric modelling** systems in which a problem to be solved in a particular region of space is decomposed into a number of simpler problems involving smaller regions of space, in order to reduce the overall complexity of the problem. A classic example is the Warnock **hidden surface removal** algorithm. See also: locality algorithms below and **VOLE** <259>.

Locality: **locality algorithms** are those that exploit some notion of local geometric properties of objects to produce candidate subproblems for **spatial decomposition** techniques in an 'intelligent' manner. A new area of research for computational geometers, and still a nebulous concept [Tilove 80].

Null Object Detection: The problem of deciding whether a representation of an object represents the null object. Of particular importance in robotics as it is the kernel of study into (static) **interference detection** and (dynamic) **clash detection**.

Dimensional Reduction: A technique often used in geometric modelling whereby a problem in some space is rewritten in a space of lower dimensionality. For example, drawing a picture of a three-dimensional object can be regarded as a projection operator onto a two-dimensional screen. See also: **ray-casting** and set-membership classification below.

Set Membership Classification: A technique in which a test set is compared against a masking set, resulting in three subsets of the test set which are inside, on the boundary of, and outside the masking set.

Contributor: Stephen Cameron.

References

[Requicha 80]   Requicha, A.A.G.
                Representations for Rigid Solids: Theory, Methods & Systems.
                ACM Computing Survey 12, 1980.

[Requicha and Voelker 77]
                Requicha, A.A.G. and Voelker, H.B.
                Constructive Solid Geometry.
                Technical report Production Automation Project TM-25, University of
                     Rochester, 1977.

[Tilove 80a]   Tilove, R.T.
                Exploiting Spatial and Structural Locality in Geometric Modelling.
                PhD thesis, Production Automation Project, University of Rochester,
                     1980.

[Tilove 80b]   Tilove, R.T.
                Set Membership Classification: A Unified Approach to Geometric
                     Intersection Problems.
                IEEE Trans. on Computers C-29(10), 1980.

41. CONTEXT-FREE GRAMMAR

A context-free grammar is a collection of context-free **phrase structure rules**. Each such rule names a constituent type and specifies a possible expansion thereof. The standard notation is:

$$\text{lhs} \rightarrow \text{rhs}_1 \ldots \text{rhs}_n$$

where lhs names the constituent, and rhs_1 through rhs_n the expansion. Such rules are **context-free rules** because the expansion is unconditional – the environment of the constituent to be expanded is irrelevant.

A collection of such rules together with an initial symbol, usually S, is a context-free grammar. The constituents expanded (those appearing on the left hand side) are called the **non-terminals**. Those not expanded (appearing only on the right hand side) are called the **terminals**. There are two standard ways of interpreting such a grammar as specifying a language. The **rewriting interpretation** says that a grammar generates the set of strings of terminals which can be produced by the following non-deterministic method:

1. Write down the initial symbol;

2. Choose a non-terminal symbol in the string, and a rule from the grammar which expands it. Replace one instance of the non-terminal with the expansion given in the rule;

3. If no non-terminals remain in the string, the process is complete. Otherwise, go back to step 2.

The **well-formedness** interpretation actually generates trees, not strings. It simply admits to the language all singly rooted trees whose root is the initial symbol and for each of whose non-leaf nodes there is a rule in the grammar such that lhs is the node label and rhs_n are the labels of its descendants in order.

Contributor: Henry Thompson.

Reference

[Gazdar 81]   Gazdar, G.
                Phrase Structure Grammar.
                In Jacobson and Pullum (editor), *The Nature of Syntactic Representations*. Reidel, Dordrecht, 1981.

42. CONTOUR GENERATOR

A Contour Generator is a set of points on a generating object surface that projects to an **occluding contour** in an image. A special case of a contour generator is an extremal boundary of an object, this is a boundary along which a surface turns smoothly away from the viewer. At extremal boundaries the surface normal is perpendicular to both the line of sight and the occluding contour projected into the image.

Contributors: T P Pridmore, S R Pollard, S T Stenton.

References

[Barrow and Tenenbaum 81]
                Barrow, H.G. and Tenenbaum, J.M.
                Interpreting Line drawings as Three-Dimensional Scenes.
                Artificial Intelligence 17:75-116, 1981.

[Marr 77]   Marr, D.
                Analysis of Occluding Contour.
                Proc. Roy. Soc. Lond. B197:441-475, 1977.

43. CONTRADICTION BACKTRACING

A method to discover and correct faulty hypotheses in a theory. If a proposition that is derived from a set of hypotheses turns out to be false in terms of a **model**, the derivation can be used to identify the faulty hypotheses. Contradiction backtracing uses the trace of a **resolution <212>** proof, in which the false proposition was the goal. The proof is traced backwards from the empty clause. Each clause is **semantically evaluated** by the user or in a standard model. If it is false, the negated parent clause is considered next, and otherwise the positive parent. The substitutions that allowed the resolution steps are accumulated and applied to each following clause. The procedure will finally lead to a hypothesis which is false.

Contributor: Maarten van Someren.

Reference

[Shapiro 81]   Shapiro, E.Y.
                 An algorithm that infers theories from facts.
                 In *Proceedings of IJCAI-81*, pages 446-451.   International Joint
                     Conference on Artificial Intelligence, 1981.

44. CONTRAST SENSITIVITY FUNCTION

The contrast sensitivity function is a normalised description of a system's sensitivity to spatial frequencies in terms of the contrast required to perform some perceptual task. For detection tasks, the human C.S.F. peaks at around 3-5 cycles/deg and reaches zero at about 60 cycles/deg. See **modulation transfer function <148>**.

Contributors: T P Pridmore, S R Pollard, S T Stenton.

Reference

[Wilson and Giese 77]
                 Wilson, H.R. and Giese S.C.
                 Threshold visibility of frequence gradient patterns.
                 Vision Research 17:1177-1190, 1977.

45. CONVOLUTION

The application of a mathematical operation to each neighbourhood in an image is called convolution. The operation is defined by a "mask" specifying for each neighbourhood, how many points it contains and how the corresponding image point affects the computations. Each location in the operator mask contains a weighting value, these are multiplied by the value of the corresponding image location and the results summed to give the convolution value for that neighbourhood. Doing this for all neighbourhoods produces a new array of values. Mathematically, the convolution integral is the integrated cross product of a weighting function with an image. See **local grey-level operations <127>**.

Contributors: T P Pridmore, S R Pollard, S T Stenton.

Reference

[Frisby 79]   Frisby, J.P.
Seeing.
Oxford University Press, 1979.

46. DADO

DADO is a parallel tree-structured machine designed to provide highly significant performance improvements in the execution of large **production rule system <192>**.
The DADO machine consists of a large, (around a hundred thousand), number of processing elements, each comprising its own processor, a small amount of local RAM, and a specialised I/O switch. The processing elements are interconnected to form a complete binary tree.

Contributor: Kevin Poulter.

Reference

[Stolfo and Shaw 82]
Stolfo, J.S., and Shaw, D.E.
DADO: A Tree-Structured Machine Architecture Architecture for Production Systems.
In *AAAI-82*. AAAI, 1982.

47. DATA-DIRECTED CONTROL

Alias: **data-driven control**.

A technique for interpretation or evaluation of a set of clauses which represent constraints or equations on unknown data items. The evaluation proceeds in pseudo-parallel **breadth-first search <25>** fashion starting with those predicates where enough data items have values. These compute values which are then used in other clauses which are added to a queue for evaluation. Evaluation proceeds until no more predicates can be evaluated. Evaluation of some predicates may generate other clauses, in which case care must be taken to avoid an explosion of partially evaluated clauses. Control depends not on the initial order of the clauses, but on the order in which data items get their value.

Contributor: P.M.D. Gray.

Reference

[Elcock, McGregor and Murray 72]
Elcock, E.W., McGregor J.J and Murray A.M.
Data Directed Control and Operating Systems.
Computer Journal :125-129, May, 1972.

48. DEFAULT REASONING

A method of overcoming the problem of insufficient information. A system may be told that unless it has information to the contrary certain defaults are assumed to be true. Systems that have default information are **non-monotonic** in the logical sense: this means that by adding certain pieces of information it may be that less results are provable than before this information was known. Examples of systems utilising default reasoning are **Thnot** in **PLANNER <143>** and the negation as failure of **PROLOG <196>**. In the latter the system assumes that if it has not been told that a certain fact is true then it is false: this is the so-called **closed world assumption**. See **truth maintenance system <250>**.

Contributor: Dave Plummer.

Reference

[Nilsson 80]   Nilsson, N. J.
Principles of Artificial Intelligence.
Tioga Pub. Co., 1980, pages 408-411.

49. DEFINITE CLAUSE GRAMMARS

A DCG consists of a set of rules in a notation based on **logic programming**. Each rule is similar to a **context-free rule** , with variables to show connections between the constituents involved, and an arbitrary test or action can be appended to the rule (for example, to handle number-agreement). DCGs are an extension of the grammar-rule notation in **PROLOG <196>**, and can be used to parse a string simply by interpreting them in a manner similar to the execution of a Prolog program.

Contributor: Graeme Ritchie.

Reference

[Pereira and Warren 80]
Pereira, F. and Warren, D.H.D.
Definite Clause Grammars for Language Analysis - A Survey of the
Formalism and a Comparison with Augmented Transition Networks.
Artificial Intelligence 13: 231-278, 1980.

50. DELAYED EVALUATION

A technique for generating a piece of program as a sequence of instructions (or as a composition of functions) from a set of clauses which specify constraints on data items. The data items are represented by tokens some of which are replaced by list structures representing "recipes" or promises to construct the given items from other items. The clauses are run through an interpreter using **data-directed control <47>** which "evaluates" the predicates. Instead of producing the computed result it gives a composed function or "recipe" which can be translated into a sequence of instructions to compute the result. This technique can also be combined with **partial evaluation <171>**. The technique can also be used with a procedural program to delay the evaluation of certain function calls e.g. for database access, until a statement to print the result is encountered.

Contributor: P. M. D. Gray.

References

[Gray 70]   Gray, P. M. D.
Compiling Programs from Problem Descriptions.
Research Report, Dept. of Computing Science, University of
Aberdeen, 1970.

[Todd 76]   Todd, S. J. P.
The Peterlee Relational Test Vehicle.
IBM Systems Journal 15: 304, 1976.

51. DEMON

Alias: **antecedent theorem**, **if-added** method.

A portion of a program which is not invoked explicitly, but which lies dormant waiting for some condition(s) to occur. For example, a knowledge manipulation program might implement **inference rules** as demons. Whenever a new piece of knowledge was added, various demons would activate (which demons depends on the particular piece of data) and would create additional pieces of knowledge by applying their respective inference rules to the original piece. These new pieces could in turn activate more demons as the inferences filtered down through chains of logic. Meanwhile the main program could continue with whatever its primary task was.

Contributor: AIWORD. DOC file (online: ARPA-net).

Reference

[Nilsson 80]   Nilsson, N. J.
Principles of Artificial Intelligence.
Tioga Pub. Co., 1980,

52. DEMPSTER-SHAFER THEORY

This is a theory of evidence potentially suitable for knowledge-based systems. The system is based on "basic probabilities" which can be visualized as probability masses that are constrained to stay within the subset with which they are associated, but are free to move over every point in the subset. From these basic probabilities we can derive upper and lower probabilities (Dempster) or belief functions and plausibilities (Shafer). The means of combining basic probabilities is using Dempster's Rule which is valid given independent evidences. A position of complete ignorance about an hypothesis is represented by having an upper probability of one and a lower probability of zero. Complete certainty about the probability of an hypothesis is represented when the upper and lower probabilities are equal. The approach can suffer from high computation times, although this can be reduced when each piece of evidence confirms or denies a single proposition rather than a disjunction. The method has been extended to allow fuzzy subsets as an expression of knowledge.

Contributor: Robert Corlett.

References

[Barnett 79]   Barnett, J.A.
                 Computational Methods for a Mathematical Theory of Evidence.
                 In *IJCAI-79*. IJCAI, 1979.

[Ishizuka et al 82]
                 Ishizuka, M., Fu K.S., Yao J.T.P.
                 SPERIL: An Expert System for Damage Assessment of Existing
                    Structures.
                 In *Conference on Pattern Recognition and Image Processing*. IEEE,
                    1982.

53. DEPENDENCY DIRECTED BACKTRACKING

Alias: **selective backtracking**.

An alternative to **chronological backtracking** where the backtrack point (the choice point that control is passed back to on failure) is determined by the nature of the failure.   That is, the choice that caused the failure is undone whereas in chronological backtracking it is simply the last choice that is reconsidered.   Some of the work done since the faulty choice may be independent of that choice, and with appropriate techniques much of this work can be retained.

Contributor: Lincoln Wallen.

References

[Pereira and Porto 82]
                 Pereira, L.M. and Porto, A.
                 Selective Backtracking.
                 In Clark, K.L. and Tarnlund, S.-A. (editor), *Logic programming*.
                    Academic Press, 1982.
                 APIC Studies in Data Processing.

[Stallman and Sussman 77]
                 Stallman, R.M. and Sussman, G.J.
                 Forward reasoning and dependency-directed backtracking in a system
                    for computer-aided cicuit analysis.
                 Artificial Intelligence 9:135-196, 1977.

54. DEPTH-FIRST PARSING

Amounts to a **depth-first search** ‹55› of the tree of alternatives which arise in the parsing process.   Clearest in the context of **top-down** ‹248› parsing of a **context-free grammar** ‹41›.   Suppose our grammar includes the following rules:

    X -> Q R S
    X -> U V W

Now suppose in the course of analysing a string, we are trying to find an X, which leads us to look for a Q, which we find.   A choice then confronts us – do we look now for an R following the Q, or do we rather look for a U at the same place we found the Q?   Given the possibility of ambiguity, either or both course may succeed.   The first choice, which leads to a **backtracking parser**, is depth–first. The second choice, which leads to a **pseudo–parallel parser**, is breadth–first <25>. If candidate string was in fact ambiguous, in the depth–first case we would find Q R S X_1 U V W X_2 in that order, whereas in the breadth–first case we would find Q U R V S W X_1 X_2.

Contributor: Henry Thompson.

Reference

[Winograd 83]   Winograd, T.
                 Language as a cognitive process.
                 Addison–Wesley, 1983.

55. DEPTH–FIRST SEARCH

Alias: **chronological backtracking**.

An uninformed **graph searching** strategy which searches the graph by exploring each possible path through it until either the required solution or a previously encountered node is encountered.   The nodes are expanded in order of depth: with the deepest node expanded first and nodes of equal depth expanded in an arbitrary order.   To prevent searching of an infinite path, a depth–bound is usually fixed and nodes below this depth are never generated, thus the strategy is neither guaranteed to produce the shortest path to the solution if one exists, nor to find a solution even if one exists.

Contributor: Dave Plummer.

Reference

[Nilsson 80]   Nilsson, N.J.
                Principles of Artificial Intelligence.
                Tioga Pub. Co., 1980.

56. DETERMINISTIC PARSING

Non–determinism arises in a parsing process which proceeds on a word by word or constituent by constituent basis because of (often local) ambiguity in the grammar and lexicon.   The degree of non–determinism can therefore be reduced by expanding the focus of attention to include more than just the 'next' constituent or word. Marcus has recently generated considerable interest with the claim that a small expansion of this sort allows English to be parsed deterministically in all but a few cases and in those it is claimed that people have difficulty as well.

Marcus and others pursuing this approach employ a **stack and buffer   parsing** technique, in which words (and sometimes completed constituents) are accessed through a fixed length (typically 3 or 5 items) buffer, and partially completed constituents are held in a stack. Grammar rules are represented by **condition-action pairs**, where the conditions refer to the buffer and the stack, and the actions effect changes therein. Rules are grouped together for the purpose of activation and deactivation – only some groups of rules are active at any given time.

Strict determinism is ensured by the finiteness of the buffer and by requiring that all structures constructed at any point in the analysis must figure in the final result. It is an open question 'how much' of English, or other natural languages, can be analysed with grammars which can be parsed in this fashion.

Contributor: Henry Thompson.

Reference

[Marcus 80]   Marcus, M.
               A theory of syntactic recognition for natural language.
               MIT Press, Cambridge, 1980.

57. DIFFERENCE OF GAUSSIANS

This function is composed of the difference of two gaussian distributions and approximates del-squared-G (the laplacian of a gaussian), the operator which Marr and Hildreth proposed to be optimal for **edge detection** in images. It also describes the 'mexican hat' weighting function of the receptive fields of retinal ganglion and LGN cells. See also **laplacian <116>**, **spatial operator**.

Contributors: T P Pridmore, S R Pollard, S T Stenton.

Reference

[Marr and Hildreth 80]
               Marr, D. and Hildreth, E.
               Theory of Edge Detection.
               Proc. Roy. Soc. Lond. B207:187-217, 1980.

58. DISCRIMINATION LEARNING

If a performance system contains overly general rules, they will lead to **errors of commission** (i.e. the rule will fire when it should not). The discrimination learning method responds to such errors by comparing the **rejection context** (the situation in which the mistake was made) to a **selection context** (the last situation in which the rule applied correctly). Based on the differences it finds between the two contexts, the method creates one or more variants of the overly general rule that contain additional conditions or otherwise restrict its generality. The new rules may still be overly general, in which case the technique is applied recursively until variants are found that match only in the desired contexts. The discrimination method can learn **disjunctive concepts**, and when combined with a strengthening process to direct search through the rule space, it can deal with noise and learn heuristically useful rules despite incomplete representations.

Contributor: Pat Langley.

References

[Anderson and Kline 79]
Anderson, J. R. and Kline, P. J.
A general learning theory and its psychological implications.
In *Proceedings of IJCAI-79*. International Joint Conference on
Artificial Intelligence, 1979.

[Langley 82]   Langley, P.
Language acquisition through error recovery.
Cognition and Brain Theory , 1982.

59. DISCRIMINATION NET

Alias: Discrimination Network, Discrimination Tree, D-net.

A mechanism for allocating an input data item to its class by applying successive tests for different individual predicates: the terminal nodes of the net represent the results to be returned for the various possible sequences of predicates. A discrimination net (**D-net**) is thus a nest of IF...THEN...ELSE tests all applicable to one data item, or more formally, a binary, directed, **acyclic graph** with unary predicates at non-terminal nodes. An example of the use of a discrimination net of this basic kind is in **natural language generation** in choosing an output word for an input meaning representation. The basic mechanism can be extended by, for instance, using n-ary rather than binary graphs, with the corresponding replacement of simple feature tests by more complex branch selection functions, by the use of variables in the data item descriptions and net patterns, and by the use of sophisticated means of indexing. With such extensions, a net can be used, for example, to implement a **PLANNER**-style <143> database optimised for retrieving individual assertions.

Discrimination nets have an obvious attraction when the set of classes involved is high; but clearly a prerequisite for their effective application is being able to identify clear test sequences for data items.

Contributor: Karen Sparck Jones.

Reference

[Charniak, Riesbeck and McDermott 80]
Charniak, E. Riesbeck, C. K. and McDermott D. V.
Artificial Intelligence Programming.
Lawrence Erlbaum Associates, Hillsdale, New Jersey.   1980.

60. DISTANCE TRANSFORM

A class of transformations on binary images which assign to each pixel of an object its distance from the nearest object boundary. The actual transformation varies with the distance measure.   Simple city block type measures can be implemented using shrink operations.   Euclidean distance measures are harder to implement in parallel. The transformation is also used on lines, where the measure is some digital arc length.

The importance of such transforms arises from the assertion that any binary object can be reconstructed from the maxima of its distance function.

Contributor: Dave Reynolds.

61. DISTRIBUTED PROBLEM SOLVING

Alias: **problem reduction**.

When a problem can be divided into independent subproblems (cf problem reduction <243>, AND/OR trees) concurrent solution of them is possible and may be advantageous. For example, Kornfeld's ETHER language permits experimentation with concurrency in **heuristic search** <92>, and Smith has implemented a **contract-net** system motivated by the metaphor of manager – contractor linkage.

Contributor: Jim Doran.

References

[Davis and Smith 83]
> Davis, R. and Smith, R. G.
> Negotiation as a Metaphor for Distributed Problem Solving.
> *Artificial Intelligence* 20: 63–109, 1983.

[Kornfeld 79] Kornfeld, W. A.
> The Use of Parallelism to Implement a Heuristic Search.
> In *Proceedings of IJCAI–79*. International Joint Conference on
>   Artificial Intelligence, 1979.

62. DYNAMIC PROGRAMMING

Dynamic programming is a **template matching** <246> technique which allows the template to be "stretched" in a non-linear fashion to find a best fit with the input pattern. It is a general purpose technique with many applications. In speech research, it has been used for recognition of words from a limited vocabulary within spoken utterances.

Contributor: Steve Isard.

63. DYNAMIC TIME WARPING

Alias: dynamic programming in speech recognition.

Two programs are provided, one that generates **lpc** and autocorrelation coefficients from the speech utterances and the other that, using **dynamic programming**, compares the test utterance with the reference utterances and finds the best match. The method used is Constrained Endpoint with 2-to-1 range of slope.

Contributor: Andrej Ljolje.

Reference

[Rabiner et al. 78]
Rabiner, L.R., Rosenberg A.E. and Levinso, S.E.
Considerations in Dynamic Time Warping Algorithms for Discrete Word
Recognition.
IEEE Trans. ASSP 26(6):575, 1978.

64. EARLEYS ALGORITHM

The first published algorithm to bring the worst case asymptotic time complexity of **recognition** for unrestricted **context-free grammars** down to cubic order in the number of words in the string to be parsed. Makes use of a **well-formed substring table**.

Contributor: Henry Thompson.

Reference

[Earley 70]
Earley, J.
An Efficient Context-Free Parsing Algorithm.
CACM 13(2):94-102, 1970.

65. EDGE DETECTION

The purpose of edge detection is to locate places in images which correspond to informative scene events, such as a shadow or the obscuring boundary of an object. The projection of such events often produces steep gradients and discontinuities in image intensity, so the basic methods of edge detection are:

- differentiate the image and threshold the resulting gradient image

- differentiate the image twice and find the **zero-crossings** in the second derivative

- **template matching** ‹246›

Computationally, this normally involves **convolution** ‹45› of a neighbourhood operator with the image at every point in the image. Very many operators have been implemented, but because of the difficulty of precisely specifying the goal of edge detection, it is difficult to compare operator performance. The latest theories of edge detection involve applying operators to the same image at different resolutions in **resolution cones** in an attempt to provide a better description of the intensity changes present in the image.

Contributor: Bob Beattie.

34

Reference

[Marr and Hildreth 80]
Marr, D. and Hildreth, E.
Theory of edge detection.
Proc. R. Soc. Lond. B207: 187–217, 1980.

66. EMYCIN

An **expert system** shell implemented in **INTERLISP** <103>. EMYCIN is a domain-independent version of **MYCIN**, a **production rule system** <192> designed for medical consultations. Problem-specific knowledge is represented as production rules where the antecedent is effectively a boolean function of predicates of attribute-object-value triples and both the **condition** and **action** have a certainty value associated with them. Uses a **backward chaining** control strategy. Incorporates a sophisticated front-end to handle user interactions and facilities for explaining how conclusions were reached and answering questions.

Contributor: Luis Jenkins.

References

[van Melle, Shortliffe and Buchanan 81]
van Melle, W., Shortliffe, E. H. and Buchanan, B.G.
9. Volume 3: *EMYCIN: A Domain-Independent System that Aids in Constructing Knowledge-Based Consultation Programs.*
Infotech State of the Art Report, 1981, .

[Waterman and Hayes-Roth 82]
Waterman, D. and Hayes-Roth, F.
An Investigation of Tools for Building Expert Systems.
Technical Report R-2818-NSF, Rand Corporation, June, 1982.

67. ENVISIONING

Envisioning is a particular kind of **qualitative reasoning**. The theory of envisioning has two principal characteristics, firstly it can be used to predict the qualitative behaviour of devices, and secondly it is a theory of causality that can be used to produce causal explanations acceptable to humans.

Envisioning produces a causal explanation for the behaviour of a physical system by explaining how disturbances from equilibrium propagate. (Envisioning should not be confused with qualitative simulation, which constitutes envisioning only in its most degenerate form).

Contributor: Kevin Poulter.

References

[de Kleer and Brown 81]
        de Kleer, J., and Brown, J.S.
        Mental Models of Physical Mechanisms and their Acquisition.
        In *Cognitive Skills and their Acquisition,* . Erlbaum, 1981.

[de Kleer and Brown 82]
        de Kleer, J., and Brown, J.S.
        Foundations of Envisioning.
        In *Proceedings of the AAAI.* AAAI, 1982.

68. EXPERT

A programming system for building **expert systems** based on classification problems, written in FORTRAN. Has been used primarily to develop models in medicine. Knowledge is represented in hypotheses, findings and decision rules with confidence factors. Evaluates its rules in an ordered manner, rather than relying on **backward chaining**. Incorporates useful front-end facilities for user-interaction.

Contributor: Luis Jenkins.

References

[Waterman and Hayes-Roth 82]
        Waterman, D. and Hayes-Roth, F.
        An Investigation of Tools for Building Expert Systems.
        Technical Report R-2818-NSF, Rand Corporation, June, 1982.

[Weiss and Kulikowski 79]
        Weiss, S.M. and Kulikowski, C.A.
        EXPERT: A System for Developing Consultation Models.
        In *Proceedings of IJCAI-79*, pages 942-947. International Joint
          Conference on Artificial Intelligence, 1979.

69. FAST PATTERN RECOGNITION TECHNIQUES

A technique for classifying very large bit vectors either by means of special purpose hardware or software has been developed. The system operates in two phases, a 'learning' phase and a 'use' phase. During the 'learning' phase examples of bit vectors together with a classifications are presented while during the 'use' phase unknown vectors are presented to the system and classified. The technique used is based on the Bledsoe and Browning n-tuple methodology.

Contributor: Igor Aleksander.

Reference

[Aleksander and Stonham 79]
        Aleksander, I and Stonham T.J.
        A Guide To Pattern Recognition Using Random-Access Memories.
        IEEE Journal of Computers & Digital Techniques 2(1), 1979.

70. FINDING COMMON PATHS

In the **production system** <192> framework, one method of generalization involves replacing constant terms with variables. However, this can lead to unbound variables in the action side, and it is desirable to include additional conditions in the generalised rule which will instantiate these variables. Suppose the generalization resulted from two rules with identical forms but differing constant terms. If one also has a long-term declarative memory available, then one can search through this memory for relations between differing symbols in the action sides of the specific rules and differing symbols in their condition sides. If analogous paths through the memory can be found for the two rules, a generalised path is created (again by replacing differing constants with variables) and this path is added as a set of conditions to the generalised rule. These conditions guarantee that all variables mentioned in the action side will be bound in the condition side. This method can be used to learn rules for solving algebra problems, for finding mappings between simple sentences and their meanings, and for discovering simple mathematical relations.

Contributor: Pat Langley.

Reference

[Langley 80]   Langley, P.
               Finding common paths as a learning mechanism.
               In *Proc. of the Third Nat. Conf.*. The Canadian Soc for
               Computational Studies of Intelligence, 1980.

71. FLYNN CLASSIFICATION

A classification for parallel computers first proposed by Flynn in which parallelism in the instruction execution and parallelism in the data handling are regarded as separate. Thus a cellular array of processors which each execute the same instruction on different data is classed as an SIMD machine (**"serial instruction – multiple data stream"**). Whereas a **pipeline** of processors performing different operations on a single stream of data could be regarded as MISD (**"multiple instruction – serial data stream"**).

Contributor: Dave Reynolds.

Reference

[Flynn 72]   Flynn M.J.
              Some Computer Organisations and their Effectiveness.
              IEEE Trans. on Computers C-21:948, 1972.

72. FOCUSSING

A technique utilised by **concept learning** programs to record knowledge about the concept that is being learnt and to facilitate the updating of this knowledge as more information becomes available to the program. For this method the description space must consist of a number of attributes that a given example might have. These are conceptually represented as **lattices** which may have arbitrary depth, each

branch of which represents a possible value for the attribute. The technique
records information by placing marks in these trees to indicate which parts of the
trees (ie which possible attribute values) are not included in the concept being
learnt. Upper marks indicate that all parts of the tree above the mark are definitely
outside the concept and a lower mark indicates that all parts of the tree below the
mark are definitely inside the concept. Between these marks there could be a grey
region which is the area that the program is uncertain about. As the program
gains more information the marks are moved to update the knowledge. Once the
upper and lower marks on all of the description trees coincide, the concept is
completely specified and the program can report completion. The program can also
detect failure if the marks become crossed (ie a lower mark above an upper one).
This technique can handle most conjunctive concepts well but encounters difficulty
handling disjunction, these difficulties may be surmountable by using multiple copies
of the description space (cf. **version space <256>**).

Contributor: Dave Plummer.

References

[Bundy and Silver 82]
Bundy, A. and Silver, B.
A critical survey of rule learning programs.
In *Proceedings of ECAI-82*, pages 150-157. European Conference
on Artificial Intelligence, 1982.

[Young, Plotkin and Linz 77]
Young, R.M., Plotkin, G.D. and Linz, R.F.
Analysis of an extended concept-learning task.
In *Proceedings of IJCAI-77*, pages 285. International Joint
Conference on Artificial Intelligence, 1977.

73. FORMANT

The formants are the principal resonances of the vocal tract, that determine
which overtones of the fundamental larynx frequency will be allowed to pass through
into the speech signal, and which will be damped. Each position of the articulators
- the lips, tongue, jaw, etc. - gives rise to a characteristic pattern of formants.
A speech signal can be represented in terms of formant patterns which change over
time, both for purposes of recognition and **synthesis-by-rule**.

Contributor: Steve Isard.

74. FORMANT SYNTHESIS

Basic sounds of a language can be characterized by their **formant <73>**
frequencies. The formant pattern for a synthetic utterance can be created by
interpolating between the formant values of the sounds composing the desired
utterance. A speech wave can be computed from such a formant pattern, to be
played through a digital-to-analogue converter, or the formant pattern can be used
directly to excite a set of resonators, acting as an electrical analogue of the vocal
tract.

Contributor: Steve Isard.

75. FORTRAN

FORTRAN is the programming Language considered by many to be the natural successor to **LISP** <34> and **Prolog** <196> for A.I. research. Its advantages include:

1. it is very efficient for numerical computation (many A.I. programs rely heavily on number-crunching techniques).

2. A.I. problems tend to be very poorly structured, meaning that control needs to move frequently from one part of a program to another. FORTRAN provides a special mechanism for achieving this, the so-called **GOTO statement**.

3. FORTRAN provides a very efficient data structure, the **array**, which is particularly useful if, for example, one wishes to process a collection of English sentences each of which has the same length.

Contributor: Martin Merry.

76. FORWARD/BACKWARD SEARCH

Alias: **data-driven/goal-directed** search, **bottom-up/top-down** search.

A **state space** <240> can be searched from the initial state to the goal state (applying **operators** <164> forward) or from the goal to the initial state (backward). In the latter case, the goal is reduced to a set of subgoals.

Contributor: Maarten van Someren.

Reference

(Barr and Feigenbaum 81)
Barr, A. and Feigenbaum, E.A. (editors).
The Handbook of Artificial Intelligence Vol. 1.
Kaufmann, 1981.

77. FRAME

Alias: **script, schema**.

Principle for the large-scale organisation of knowledge introduced by Minsky, originally in connection with vision, but generally applicable. A simple example is the GUS air trip frame, a structure with slots for the various elements of a trip e.g. passenger, source, destination, date, etc. which are instantiated in any particular application of the frame. Frames may be arbitrarily complex, and have procedures attached to the slots. Default values for the slots are helpful when frames are exploited in the absence of full instantiation data. The character of frames suggests a hierarchical organisation of sets of frames, but non-hierarchical filling of one frame slot by another is possible. Frame structures are often not deemed to imply temporal or causal relations between their slots, and are thus contrasted with **scripts** <223> but community usage in this respect is very inconsistent: one man's frame is another man's script, and vice versa. The main problem with systems with multiple frames is frame selection and replacement.

Contributor: Karen Sparck Jones.

Reference

[Minsky 75]   Minsky, M.
               A framework for representing knowledge.
               In P.H. Winston (editor), *The Psychology of Computer Vision*.
                   McGraw-Hill, 1975.

78. FRL

Alias: Frames Representation Language.

FRL is a knowledge representation language based on **frames** <77>. Each "frame" has a certain number of "slots", each with a number of "facets". Each "datum" (facet entry) can have attached a list of "comments", where each comment consists of some label or keyword followed by a list of "messages". FRL allows **procedural attachment** <188>; three of the six standard facet names being "if-added", "if-removed", and "if-needed". FRL is implemented as an interpreter written in **LISP** <34>.

Contributor: Robert Corlett.

Reference

[Roberts and Goldstein 77]
               Roberts, R.E., and Goldstein, I.P.
               The FRL Manual
               AI Memo 409 edition, MIT AI Lab., 1977.

79. FUNCTIONAL DATA MODEL

An **entity-relationship data model** with relationships expressed as functions which map their arguments to a single entity value or to a set of entities. Derived functions allow the definition of arbitrary new relationships in terms of existing ones. Different user views of data can be presented by defining appropriate derived functions. Updating of derived relationships is supported through procedures explicitly provided by the user.

Data manipulation languages, such as **DAPLEX**, have been added to the Functional Data Model to provide the notion of looping through entity sets to perform operations.

The Functional data model incorporates many of the ideas in earlier **semantic net** <227> systems, the **if-needed** and **if-added** theorems of the **PLANNER** <143> and **CONNIVER** <38> languages, and a range of data models.

Contributor: Austin Tate.

Reference

[Shipman 81]   Shipman, D.W.
               The Functional Data Model and the Data Language DAPLEX.
               ACM Transactions and Database Systems 6(1):140-173, 1981.

80. FUNCTIONAL GRAMMAR

Functional grammar is a declarative expression of the relation between **surface structure** and **functional structure** in a natural language which is equally suitable for use in **parsing** and **generation**. The functional structure is a **directed acyclic graph** of attributes and values indicating the functional roles played by sentence constituents, e.g. subject, modifier ... Functional grammar has been adopted by a number of language generation systems as their grammatical basis.

Contributor: Henry Thompson.

References

[Appelt 83]   Appelt, D.E.
               Telegram: a Grammar Formalism for Language Planning.
               In *Proceedings of the 21st Annual Meeting of the Association for
                   Computational Linguistics*. Association for Computational
                   Linguistics, 1983.

[Kay 79]   Kay, M.
               Functional Grammar.
               In *Proceedings of the Fifth Annual Meeting of the Berkeley Linguistic
                   Society*. Berkeley Linguistic Society, 1979.

81. FUZZY RELATIONAL PRODUCTS

Special non-symmetrical products of **fuzzy relations** (binary or higher n-ary) to allow formation of structures of increasing complexity, and parallel processing of them. Applications include implementation of extended **semantic nets <227>** and a curtailment of rule-based inference.

Contributor: L.J. Kohout.

Reference

[Bandler and Kohout 80]
               Bandler, W and Kohout, L.J.
               Fuzzy Relational Products as a Tool for Analysis and Synthesis of the
                   Behaviour of Complex Artificial and Natural Systems.
               In *Fuzzy sets: Theory and Applications to Policy Analysis and
                   Information Systems*, pages 341-367.". PlenumPress, 1980.

82. FUZZY SET THEORY

Alias: **fuzzy logic**.

An extension of conventional set theory, with the grade of membership for an element in a set taking a value anywhere in the range [0, 1], instead of 0 or 1 only. Developed as a means of avoiding the complexity in descriptions of subjective or ill-understood processes. Fuzzy logic extends the simple Boolean operators and can express implication.

Contributor: Janet Efstathiou.

<u>References</u>

[Mamdani and Gaines 81]
        Mamdani, E. H. and Gaines, B. R.
        Fuzzy Reasoning and its Applications.
        Academic Press, London, 1981.

[Zadeh 73]   Zadeh, L. A.
        Outline of a new approach to the analysis of complex systems and
           decision processes.
        IEEE Trans. of Systems, Man and Cybernetics SMA-3: 28-44, 1973.

83. GENERALISED CYLINDERS

Alias: **generalised cone**.

A currently popular method for three-dimensional **shape description**. Generalised cylinders are a class of objects obtained by extending the definition of a cylinder. An ordinary cylinder is the volume swept out by a circular disc moving perpendicular to a straight line segment that passes through its center called the axis or spine of the cylinder. A generalised cylinder is then obtained by extending the definition to include things like:

1. A curved spine.

2. The radius of the disc varying as a function of the position along the spine.

3. The cross section being some planar figure other than a circle.

4. The cross section held at a non-perpendicular angle to the spine.

Contributor: Luis Jenkins.

<u>References</u>

(Cohen and Feigenbaum 82)
        Cohen, P. and Feigenbaum, E. (editors).
        The Handbook of Artificial Intelligence Vol. 3.
        Kaufmann, 1982.

[Marr 77]   Marr, D.
        Analysis of occluding contour.
        Proc. Roy. Soc. London B197, 1977.

84. GENERALISED HOUGH TRANSFORM

The Hough transform technique was originally a method for detecting, in images, lines and other shapes characterisable by analytic functions. It has recently been extended (primarily by Ballard) to handle the correlation of 2D and 3D shapes which have no analytic description. One way of describing the technique is as a mapping from a spatially indexed **feature space** to a non-spatially indexed **parameter space** for the purpose of **scene segmentation**. The **image segmentation** technique of histogramming-then-thresholding can be used as an illustration. A very crude, and only under special circumstances successful, segmentation technique is to create a histogram of **grey-level image** intensity levels, ie. map the spatially indexed intensity values into a non-spatially indexed intensity **grey level feature space**. If the image originally consisted of an object and background of very different average reflectance properties, the histogram may have two clearly defined peaks. Simple thresholding at the minimum between them may suffice to segment figure from ground. Extending this idea to a colour feature space one can see that points contributing to peaks in the non-spatially indexed colour space may originate from significant spatially extended segments of the image, the blue of the sky, the green of the grass, the red roofs etc. Yet another example: consider the optic flow or instantaneous velocity image, grouping the points that are all moving in the same direction with the same velocity may be sufficient to segment out of the image the onrushing traffic from the background, etc. etc.

One of the reasons why the simple histogramming of intensity levels is rarely successful as a segmentation technique, except under controlled lighting and other application specific conditions, is that the grey level intensity values are only indirectly related to surface characteristics. They confound the reflectance of the surface, its orientation, and the direction of the illumination. It is for this reason that the **intrinsic images** <105> ie. images explicitly portraying "intrinsic" surface characteristics, are a much more suitable representation from which to compute a description of the scene. One of the important contributions of Ballard and his colleagues is that they have developed and extended the idea behind the simple histogramming technique into a "specification of an abstract computational machine" capable of exploiting the recent theoretical advances in the intrinsic image computations. They propose the GHT, not only as a way of utilising the information carried by the intrinsic images for higher level scene description and segmentation, but also to couple the computations between intrinsic images using **shared parameter spaces**, and even to compute the intrinsic image features.

A fundamental strand in the approach is what has been called "connectionist modelling". The fundamental tenet of CM is that neurones in the brain compute, "not by transmitting large amounts of symbolic information but by being appropriately connected to large numbers of similar units" (Feldman and Ballard 1982). When they say large numbers they mean it. The number of units that could be required in a multidimensional feature space is exponential in the number of dimensions. If N is the number of units needed to span the range of values in a feature space, a D dimensional feature space requires N^D units. There are two schemes proposed to bring the number of units required down to reasonable numbers: 1) Coarse coding: this is an idea that the brain also seems to use. Instead of using a single high resolution unit to signal a value in a feature space, the output of several overlapping low resolution units can localise the value with equivalent resolution but considerable savings in the number of units required. Many children's magic "choose a symbol" tricks work like this. 2) Feature space decompositions: It is often possible to decompose a D dimensional space into two D/2 dimensional spaces, and use the maxima in one subspace to facilitate processing in the other. eg. the GHT for 2D pattern recognition can be regarded as a 4D parameter space: rotation(r), scaling(s), and translation (x, y). [Ballard and Sabbah 1980] show that it may be treated serially as two 2D parameter spaces, (r, s) and (x, y). Two 2D spaces require many fewer units than one 4D space. The process works because each subspace is a projection of the whole space. A way of improving the effectiveness of feature space decomposition is to mask off the inputs that do not contribute to the peaks in the first parameter space; this helps to overcome the blurring that can arise due to the fact that each subspace is a projection of a space of greater dimensionality and will thus "sharpen" the projection in the second parameter space. This strategy of masking out inputs based on values in one or more parameter spaces is quite general in application, it also corresponds very well to a psychological phenomenon known as **partial report**.

Contributor: Jon Mayhew.

Reference

[Ballard 82]   Ballard D.
                Parameter Nets.
                Technical Report 75 revised, Computer Science Dept., University of
                    Rochester NY., 1982.

85. GENERATIVE CAPACITY

Generative capacity is a characteristic of grammatical formalisms. **Weak generative capacity** refers to the kind of languages a formalism can characterise purely in terms of their **string set** - that is, in terms of the strings of items which are members of the language. **Strong generative capacity** is a less clear-cut notion which refers not just to strings but also to structures.

Contributor: Henry Thompson.

Reference

[Hopcroft and Ullman 79]
                Hopcroft, J.E. and Ullman, J.D.
                Introduction to Automata Theory, Languages, and Computation.
                Addison Wesley, 1979.

86. GOAL STRUCTURE

Alias: **holding periods, plan kernels**.

Information about a plan which represents the purpose of the various plan parts in terms of the goals or subgoals they are intended to achieve. This can be contrasted with the **Plan Structure** <180> which contains details which may obscure information important to the finding of causes for planning or execution failures.

The **STRIPS MACROPS** (**operator tables** <163>) used such information for plan execution. Goal Structure has been used in a linear planner (**INTERPLAN**) and a **non-linear planner** (**NONLIN**) to guide search. It can be viewed as a **Meta-planning** <140> technique.

Contributor: Austin Tate.

References

[Fikes]   Fikes, R. E.
                Knowledge Representation in Automatic Planning Systems.
                Technical Note 119, SRI,

[Tate 75]   Tate, A.
                Using Goal Structure to direct search in a Problem Solver.
                PhD thesis, MIRU, Edinburgh, 1975.

[Tate 76]   Tate, A.
                Project Planning using a Hierarchic Non-Linear Planner.
                Research Report 25, DAI, 1976.

87. GOLAY NEIGHBOURHOODS

A set of local patterns, devised by Golay for transformations on hexagonally connected **binary images**. They fall into the general class of **morphological transforms** ("hit or miss"). Each pattern is a hexagon of "true", "false" and "do not care" entries. When a pattern matches the neighbourhood of a pixel in the image that pixel can be marked (to detect special points like line ends), set true (to "thicken" the image) or set false (to "thin" or "skeletonise" the image). See **local grey-level operations** <127>.

Generalisations of such operations are now used for processing images with square connectivity.

Contributor: Dave Reynolds.

Reference

[Golay 69]   Golay M. J. E.
                Hexagonal Parallel Pattern Transformations.
                IEEE Transactions on Computers C-18(8), 1969.

88. GRADIENT SPACE

A two dimensional space used to represent surface orientation in terms of its vertical and horizontal components. Thus the plane surface $-Z = P.X + Q.Y + C$ is represented by the point (P, Q) in gradient space. The steepness of the surface is squareroot($P^2 + Q^2$) and the direction of the slope is $\tan^{-1}(Q/P)$. Such a representation does not make explicit the spatial location or extent of surface planes. Convex and concave edges and curvatures will be represented by lines in the gradient space, in the case of planar surface discontinuity edges these will be perpendicular to the edge in the image space, with order along the line determined by the convexity/concavity.

Contributors: T P Pridmore, S R Pollard, S P Stenton.

Reference

[Draper 81]   Draper, S. W.
               The Use of Gradient Space and Dual Space in Line Drawing
                    Interpretation.
               Artificial Intelligence 17, 1981.

89. GREY-LEVEL IMAGE

The grey-level image is a point-by-point representation of image intensities, formed by the optical image triggering various photochemical and/or photoelectric processes. It is pointilliste, making explicit only local intensity values; all other information is left implicit.

Contributors: T P Pridmore, S R Pollard, S P Stenton.

Reference

[Frisby 79]   Frisby, J. P.
               Seeing.
                Oxford Uni. Press, 1979.

90. HETERARCHY

In a **pipelined <177>** or **hierarchical process organisation**, image data passes through a sequence of analytical or interpretive modules each of which acts independently of the rest. In a **heterarchical system**, modules may invoke other modules in the series to help with e.g. disambiguation of data. Winograd's program **SHRDLU**, in which syntactic analysis could make use of semantic modules on knowledge about the world was the most famous example. Shirai and others designed heterarchic image understanding programs. Heterarchy fell into disrepute when the work of Horn, Barrow and Tenenbaum suggested that far more disambiguation can be done autonomously by low levels than was previously thought. The fashion will change again when it is realised that in poor viewing conditions more sophisticated process organisation is required.

Contributor: Aaron Sloman.

Reference

[Clowes]   Clowes, M. B.
Man the creative machine.
In J. Benthall (editor), *The limits of human nature*.

91. HEARSAY-III

A domain-independent programming facility for developing prototype **expert** systems, evolved from work on speech understanding. A **blackboard <19>** is used to store and coordinate information about the domain and state of computation and most of the domain-specific knowledge is organized in complex **production rules <192>** called **knowledge sources** (KS). The general-purpose control structure supports interaction among numerous and diverse sources of knowledge and competing subproblems.

Contributor: Luis Jenkins.

References

[Balzer et al 80]Balzer, R., Erman, L.D., London, P. and Williams, C.
HEARSAY-II: A Domain-Independent Framework for Expert Systems.
In *Proc. First Annual National Conference on Artificial Intelligence*,
pages 108-110. American Association for Artificial Intelligence,
1980.

[Waterman and Hayes-Roth 82]
Waterman, D. and Hayes-Roth, F.
An Investigation of Tools for Building Expert Systems.
Technical Report R-2818-NSF, Rand Corporation, June, 1982.

92. HEURISTIC SEARCH

Alias: **best first search**.

A technique for state space searching, with the **state space <240>** represented as a graph. It uses domain-specific knowledge expressed as a numerical **evaluation function** which assigns a number to each node of the graph. At each stage of the search, heuristic search develops the tip node with the best numeric score. Tip nodes may be stored on an **agenda** in order of numeric score.

Contributor: Dave Plummer.

Reference

[Nilsson 80]   Nilsson, N.J.
Principles of Artificial Intelligence.
Tioga Pub. Co., 1980.

93. HIERARCHICAL PLANNING

Alias: **plan refinement**, top-down plan elaboration.

The technique by which a hierarchical plan structure is generated by successive generation, from top to bottom, of its component levels. One variant of the technique [Sacerdoti 78] makes use of **criticalities** assigned to operator preconditions. More generally, domain specific **plan elaboration rules** are required [Tate 77]. Top-down plan elaboration is closely related to automatic top-down programming techniques [Barstow 79] (see PECOS within PSI <201>).

Contributor: Jim Doran.

References

[Barstow 79]   Barstow, D. R.
                 An experiment in knowledge-based automatic programming.
                 Artificial Intelligence 12: 73-119, 1979.

[Sacerdoti 78]   Sacerdoti, E. D.
                 Planning in a hierarchy of abstraction spaces.
                 Artificial Intelligence 5: 115-135, 1978.

[Tate 77]   Tate, A.
                 Generating Project Networks.
                 In *Proceedings of IJCAI-77.* International Joint Conference on
                     Artificial Intelligence, 1977.

94. HIGH-EMPHASIS FILTERING

A method for sharpening images. The differentiation of an image is grossly interpreted in the frequency domain as filtering that emphasizes higher frequency components. As any linear operator in the spatial domain can be converted into an equivalent **transfer function** in the frequency domain, a linear operator designed to emphasize abrupt changes in intensity can be implemented by a transfer function designed to emphasize areas of high frequency.

Contributor: Luis Jenkins.

Reference

(Cohen and Feigenbaum 82)
                 Cohen, P. and Feigenbaum, E. (editors).
                 The Handbook of Artificial Intelligence Vol. 3.
                 Kaufmann, 1982.
                 pp206-215.

95. HOOK

A hook is a piece of code or data-structure in an implementation which is made available to simplify later augmentation of the system. A good example is an evaluation algorithm that leaves sufficient information on the run-time stack for a

48

good debugging package to be possible.

Contributor: Bruce Anderson.

96. HOPE

An **applicative language** designed to encourage the construction of clear and correct programs. The language is strongly typed, allowing **polymorphic types**, higher-order types and **overloaded operators**, and includes a simple but powerful type-definition facility. Functions are defined by a set of recursion equations; the left-hand side of each equation includes a pattern used to determine which equation to use for a given argument. Additional features include a simple modularisation facility and **lazy lists** (**streams**). Currently an experimental, rather slow implementation is available.

Contributor: Mike Gordon.

Availability

Available as a research tool with documentation and informal support.

Environment: DEC10 (with POP2), VAX (with Franzlisp)

From: John Scott,
      Department of Computer Science,
      Edinburgh University,
      JCMB, King's Buildings,
      Mayfield road,
      Edinburgh,
      Scotland.

      Tel: (031) 667-1081

Reference

[Burstall, MacQueen and Sannella 80]
      Burstall, R.M., MacQueen, D.B and Sannella, D.T.
      HOPE: an experimental applicative language.
      In *Proc. 1980 LISP Conference, Stanford, California*, pages 136-143.
      1980.

97. HORN CLAUSES

Horn Clauses are formulae of first order **predicate calculus <189>** of the form:

A1 & A2 & ... & An -> A   or   A1 & A2 & ... & An ->

where each of the Ai and A are atomic formulae i.e. of the form R(C1,...,Cn), where R is a **relation**, each Cj is a **term**, and $n \geq 0$.

They have several important properties when viewed from **mathematical logic**.

(See **clausal form** <33>) In addition, they form the basis for the **logic programming** language **PROLOG** <196>: each predicate in a Prolog program has a horn clause definition.   The above formulae would be written

A :- A1,A2,...,An.   and ?- A1,A2,...An.

respectively as Prolog programs.

Contributor: Martin Merry.

<u>References</u>

[Chang and Keisler 73]
               Chang, C.C. and Keisler, H.J.
               Model Theory.
               North-Holland, 1973.

[Kowalski 79]   Kowalski, R.A.
               Logic for problem solving.
               North-Holland, 1979.

98. IMAGE DATA STRUCTURES

A wide variety of data structures are used to represent images.   At the low level, raw **grey level** <89> or binary images are represented by arrays of **pixels** (with square, triangular or hexagonal connectivity).   Object boundaries are described by **fourier descriptors** or strings (Freeman chain code, symbolic strings).   The adjacency of object regions is described by graph structures such as the **region adjacency graph**.   Finally hierarchical or **pyramidal** <202> data structures which describe an image at a series of different levels or resolutions have proved useful (eg. **quad trees** <204>).

Contributor: Dave Reynolds.

<u>Reference</u>

[Tanimoto and Klinger 80]
               Tanimoto S. and Klinger A.
               Structured Computer Vision.
               Academic Press, New York, 1980.

99. IMAGE SEGMENTATION

Segmentation (in the context of image processing) is the action of splitting a **grey-level image** into meaningful subsets.   For example a useful segmentation of a blood smear picture would detect each blood cell as a single object. This can generally be performed by low level processes or high level processes. **Region** finding <208> and **line finding** <121> are simple examples.

Low-level segmentation is performed by grouping **pixels** according to brightness or texture similarities (local or global thresholding is a trivial example) or by looking for the edges of objects (often by means of convolution with edge like masks).

High-level segmentation generally consists of using expectations from models to guide the use of low level feature detectors.

Contributor: Dave Reynolds.

<u>References</u>

[Brady 82]   Brady, M.
              Computational approaches to image understanding.
              Computer Surveys 14, 1982.

[Fu and Mui 81]Fu K.S. and Mui J.K.
              A Survey on Image Segmentation.
              Pattern Recognition 13:3-16, 1981.

100. INFERENCE ENGINE TOOLKIT

The Inference Engine toolkit is a document on a backward-chaining inference engine toolkit, including source code in FORTH. The inference engine uses a production language syntax which allows semantic inference and access to analytical subroutines written in FORTH. Source code is included for a forward-chaining tool, but the strategy is not implemented in the inference routines. The code is available on disks formatted for a variety of personal computers.

Contributor: Jack Park .

<u>Availability</u>

From: Jack Park,
      Helion, Inc.,
      Box 445,
      Brownsville,
      CA 95919, USA.

      Tel: (916) 675-2478

101. INFERNO

Inferno is a conservative approach to uncertainty. It is based on a probabilistic approach to uncertainty, but, unlike most similar schemes, does not make any assumptions about relationships between propositions (eg. independence). It is, however, possible to assert such relationships in Inferno if they exist. The method is essentially based on upper and lower probabilities (see **Dempster-Shafer Theory**) which give upper and lower bounds on the probability of each proposition. Each time one of these bounds change, the bounds on related propositions are checked and suitably modified to satisfy a set of propagation constraints. These constraints are based on the inequality

$$\max(P(A), P(B)) \le P(A \text{ or } B) \le P(A) + P(B).$$

One unique feature of Inferno is its ability to detect and suggest corrections for contradictions and inconsistencies in its data. If, the propagation constraints cannot provide valid values for the bounds, Inferno invokes a method similar to dependency-directed backtracking <53> to suggest changes to the data that would remove the inconsistency.

Contributor: Robert Corlett.

Reference

[Quinlan 83]   Quinlan, J. R.
                Inferno: A Cautious Approach To Uncertain Inference.
                The Computer Journal 26(3), 1983.

102. INTERACTIONS BETWEEN SUB-GOALS

Whenever a planner makes the assumption that conjunctive goals can be solved independently (either one after the other or in parallel) there is likely to be interference between the partial solutions.   Techniques have been developed to recognise and correct for these interactions between solutions to conjunctive goals.

Sussman's **HACKER** solved problems by assuming an ordered solution was feasible.   It then had **critics** to recognise interactions and HACKER was often able to repair the plan by re-arranging the steps in the plan.   In his **INTERPLAN** program, Tate's approach was to abstract the original goals and to determine holding periods over which these could be assumed to be true.   INTERPLAN analysed this "goal structure" with a view towards ordering sub-goals to ease conflict situations. Waldinger developed an approach called "goal regression" in which a solution to one goal was built and then the plan was constructively modified to achieve the further plans (by moving new goals backwards through a partial plan to a position where they did not interfere).   A scheme similar to that used by Waldinger was incorporated in WARPLAN , a planner written in PROLOG <196>.

All the above mentioned planners produce their plans as a linear sequence of actions.   **Non-linear planners** <158>, NONLIN also dealt with interactions between sub-goals in plans which are produced as partially ordered networks of actions.

Contributor: Austin Tate (adapted from Mark Stefik).

References

[Sussman 75]   Sussman, G. J.
                A computational model of skill acquisition.
                American Elsevier, New York, 1975.

[Tate 79]   Tate, A.
                Interacting Goals and their use.
                In *Proceedings of IJCAI-79.*   International Joint Conference on
                    Artificial Intelligence, 1979.

[Waldinger 75] Waldinger, R.
                Achieving several goals simultaneously.
                Technical Note 107, SRI AI Center, 1975.

[Warren 74]   Warren, D. H. D.
WARPLAN: A system for generating plans.
Memo 76, Dept. of Artificial Intelligence, Edinburgh, 1974.

103. INTERLISP-D

Major dialect of **LISP <34>**, designed for high-resolution, bit-mapped display, distinguished by (a) use of in-core editor for structures, and thus code, (b) programming environment of tools for automatic error-correction, syntax (sic) extension and structure declaration/access, (c) implementation of almost-compatible dialects (Interlisp <X>) on several machines, (d) extensive usage of display oriented tools and facilities. Emphasis: Personal Lisp workstation, user interface tools.

Contributor: Martin Gittins.

Availability

Commercially available with documentation and support.

Environment: Xerox 1108 only (or 1100, 1132 in US only).

From: David Catton
Artificial Intelligence Ltd.
62-78 Merton Rd.
Watford, WD1 7BY,
England.

Tel: 0923-47707

104. INTERN DEMONS

An intern demon is a **demon <51>** which is triggered whenever an S-expression is interned which matches a given trigger pattern. Intern demons are useful in ensuring **invariants** which concern all interned assertions or terms. There is an important distinction between interning an expression and making an expression true or false (classical demons trigger when expressions are made true).

Contributor: D. McAllester.

Reference

[McAllester 82] McAllester, D.
Reasoning Utility Package User's Manual Version One.
Memo 667, MIT AI Lab, April, 1982.

105. INTRINSIC IMAGES

The term was first used by Barrow and Tenenbaum (1976) to refer to a registered "stack" of retinotopic maps each of which makes explicit the value of a certain property "intrinsic" to the surfaces in the scene. The intrinsic images all have the same viewer centred coordinate system but carry information about different surface properties, such as: surface orientation, depth, reflectance, colour, texture and optic flow (this last intrinsic image describes the instantaneous velocity flow field in the scene). The computation of the intrinsic images is non-trivial, many of them are underdetermined when considered independently but global consistency constraints can be cooperatively exploited, eg surface boundary information carried by the reflectance image can be used to constrain the computation of the surface orientation from shading information.

Over the last five years there have been considerable advances in understanding of the problems of computing the different intrinsic images. Their particular importance is that they are a vital stage in the computation of a representation intermediate between the lowest levels of image processing, whose descriptions are essentially 2D pictorial or iconic descriptions of the scene, and the higher levels of processing which describe the shapes of objects in terms of an object centred viewer independent coordinate system. The intrinsic images are the first representation at which information concerning the 3D structure of the scene is made explicit. Object recognition schemes that have attempted to recover 3D shape descriptions directly from 2D shape descriptions have, to put it mildly, struggled. See also 2 1/2-D sketch <1>.

Contributor: Jon Mayhew.

References

[Barrow and Tenenbaum 81]
Barrow, H.G. and Tenenbaum, J.M.
Computational Vision.
In *Proc IEEE 6*, pages 572-596. IEEE, 1981.

[Brady 82]   Brady, M.
Computational Approaches to Image Understanding.
Computer Surveys 14(1):2-71, 1982.

106. INVARIANT QUEUES

An **invariant** is an assertion about a data structure or database which is expected to be true at certain times. For example a **resolution** <212> data base should not contain empty clauses between queries. An invariant queue is a queue which contains at least one entry for each violation of a given invariant. Processing an entry from an invariant queue should remove a violation of the invariant. If an invariant queue is empty then the invariant should hold. A given system can have many invariants and many invariant queues.

Contributor: D. McAllester.

Reference

[McAllester 82] McAllester, D.
Reasoning Utility Package User's Manual Version One.
Memo 667, MIT AI Lab, April, 1982.

107. INVARIANT VIOLATION DEMONS

An invariant violation demon is a **demon** <51> which triggers when an **invariant** is violated. Such demons can either correct the violation immediately or place an entry on an **invariant queue**<106>.

Contributor: D. McAllester.

Reference

[McAllester 82] McAllester, D.
Reasoning Utility Package User's Manual Version One.
Memo 667, MIT AI Lab., April, 1982.

108. ISA HIERARCHY

Alias: **inheritance hierarchy, type hierarchy.**

Strictly a straightforward manifestation of class membership, found useful in knowledge representation because property specifications for classes need only be explicitly indicated once, i.e. at the highest level, since they are automatically inherited by subclasses. ISA relationships are often found in a **semantic net** <227>. This form of ISA relationship must be clearly distinguished from ISA relationships between individuals and the classes of which they are members. This second version of the ISA relationship is also found in semantic nets.

Contributor: Karen Sparck Jones.

Reference

[Fahlman 79] Fahlman, S.E.
NETL: A System for Representing and Using Real-World Knowledge.
MIT Press, 1979.

109. ISLAND PARSING

Adaptation of **augmented transition network** <14> parsing to deal with the problems presented by e.g. speech where the terminal symbols of the grammar cannot be certainly identified in correct linear sequence in the input. Bidirectional parsing is initiated from any plausibly identified node in the network, an island, providing hypotheses to assist the identification of uncertain input items. However parsing is complicated by the fact that tests and actions may be context dependent, and may not be executable because the required information for leftward input items is not yet available.

Contributor: Karen Sparck Jones.

Reference

[Woods 76]   Woods, W. et al.
Speech Understanding Systems, Final Report Vol. 4.
Report 3438, Beranek and Newman Inc., 1976.

110. JUNCTION DICTIONARY

Within the **blocks world** domain, only a restricted set of edge types of vertices, and thus line junctions in the image, exist. A junction dictionary can be constructed for line labellings of each member of this set. Of all the possible line labellings, that imply a potentially large dictionary, only a small subset are in fact physically possible. See also **relaxation labelling <210>** and **line labelling <122>**.

Contributors: T P Pridmore, S R Pollard, S P Stenton.

Reference

[Waltz 75]   Waltz, D.
Understanding Line Drawings of Scenes with Shadows.
In P.H. Winston (editor), *The Psychology of Computer Vision.*
McGraw-Hill, 1975.

111. KAS: KNOWLEDGE ACQUISITION SYSTEM

An **expert systems** building tool written in **INTERLISP <103>**. KAS is the Knowledge Acquisition System of **Prospector**, a consultation program for mineral exploration. Knowledge can be represented in two basic ways, probabilistic **inference rules** and partitioned **semantic networks <227>**. Control is via both **forward chaining** and **backward chaining**. Incorporates a sophisticated front-end with useful facilities for I/O, data base construction and explanation.

Contributor: Luis Jenkins.

References

[Reboh 79]   Reboh, R.
The Knowledge Acquisition System.
In Duda, R.O. (editor), *A Computer-Based Consultant for Mineral Exploration.* SRI International, Artificial Intelligence Center, Menlo Park, September, 1979.
Final Report, SRI Project 6415.

[Waterman and Hayes-Roth 82]
Waterman, D. and Hayes-Roth, F.
An Investigation of Tools for Building Expert Systems.
Technical Report R-2818-NSF, Rand Corporation, June, 1982.

112. KINEMATICS

Analysis of the kinematics of mechanisms can provide a technique for rational design of manipulators and workspaces. Mechanical arrangements for robot manipulators vary widely among operational robots, the most common configurations being best described in terms of their coordinate features: cartesian, spherical, and articulated. In a cartesian robot, a wrist is mounted on a rigid framework to permit linear movement along three orthogonal axes, rather like a gantry crane or (for two axes) a graph plotter; the resulting workspace is box-shaped. The cylindrical robot has a horizontal arm mounted on a vertical column which is fixed to a rotating base. The arm moves in and out; a carriage moves the arm up and down along the column, and these two components rotate as a single element on the base; the workspace is a portion of a cylinder. The spherical robot is similar to the turret of a tank: the arm moves in and out, pivots vertically, and rotates horizontally about the base; the workspace is a portion of a sphere. An articulated robot is more anthropomorphic: an upper arm and forearm move in a vertical plane above a rotating trunk. The limbs are connected by revolute joints; the workspace approximates a portion of a sphere. For all robots, additional degrees of freedom are provided at the extremity of the arm, at the wrist. Wrists generally allow rotation in two or three orthogonal planes. To make proper use of a robot arm, transformations between encoded axis values (joint angles, etc) and more convenient coordinate systems must be computed at high speed. Transforming a set of axis values to a position and orientation in space is called the forward kinematics transformation. The reverse transformation is used to convert a desired position and orientation in space into commanded axis values.

Contributor: W.F. Clocksin.

References

[Engleberger 80] Engleberger J.F.
                 Robotics in Practice.
                 IFS Publications, 1980.

[Paul 81]   Paul R.P.
                 Robot Manipulators.
                 MIT Press, 1981.

[Simons 80]   Simons G.L.
                 Robots in Industry.
                 NCC Publications, 1980.

113. KL-ONE/KL-TWO

KL-ONE and KL-TWO are programming systems for representing and manipulating knowledge. They have been in development at BBN during the late 1970s. KL-ONE is an outgrowth of the **semantic net** <227> school of representation, and includes some of the features of Minsky's **frames** <77>. Classes are represented by "Concepts" (similar to frames), and their properties are represented by "roles" (similar to slots of frames). Concepts and roles are organized into separate taxonomies based on the relation of subsumption (similar to ISA) (see **ISA hierarchy** <108>), giving a notion of sub- and super-Concepts, as well as sub- and super-Roles. There is a system of inheritance by which Concepts (and Roles) acquire attributes of their super-Concepts (and super-Roles), and there is an algorithm, called classification, that discovers appropriate subsumption relationships that are not explicitly stated. A formal specification of the semantics of KL-ONE has been given [Sidner et al 83] in which one-place predicates are associated with Concepts and two-place predicates with Roles, where the predicates may be complex. A new system, called KL-TWO, includes KL-ONE plus a separate component for asserting facts about individuals. This component provides a propositional calculus with equality where Concepts and Roles may be used as one- and two-place predicates respectively.

Contributor: James Schmolze.

Availability

Available with documentation.

Environment: Interlisp

From: James G. Schmolze (non-commercial)
Bob Harvey (commercial),
BBN Laboratories,
10 Moulton St.,
Cambridge,
MA 02238,
USA

Tel: 617-491-1850
Electronic Address: schmoltze@bbn (Arpanet)

References

[Brachman 77] Brachman, R.J.
A Structural Paradigm for Representing Knowledge.
PhD thesis, Harvard University, 1977.

[Brachman and Schmolze ??]
Brachman, R.J. and Schmolze, J.G.
An Overview of the KL-ONE Knowledge Representation System.
To appear in Cognitive Science. Expected in 1985.

[Sidner et al 83]
Sidner, C.L., Bates, M., Bobrow, R., Goodman, B., Haas, A.,
Ingria, R., McAllester, D., Moser, M., Schmolze, J., Vilain, M.
*Research in Knowledge Representation for Natural Language
Understanding - Annual Report, 1September 1982 - 31 August
1983*.
Technical Report 5421, BBN Laboratories, 1983.

114. KRC

A higher-order applicative language developed at the University of Kent by David Turner. Based on earlier language **SASL** <222>, but with addition of powerful notation for set abstraction and improved interactive facilities for program development (built-in editor etc). Like SASL makes full use of lazy evaluation, permitting free-wheeling use of infinite data structures. Current version is weakly typed, but about to be replaced by successor language incorporating polymorphic strong typing.

58

Contributor: D.A. Turner.

Reference

[Turner 82]   Turner, D.A.
               Recursion Equations as a Programming Language.
               In *Functional Programming and its Applications,* .   CUP, 1982.

115. KRL

Alias: **knowledge representation language**.

During the late 1970s, various research workers at Stanford University and Xerox
PARC developed a set of **INTERLISP** programs which embodied many of the ideas of
Minsky's **frames** <77>, together with facilities for matching structures against each
other and for controlling multi-processing.   Although "KRL" stood for "Knowledge
Representation Language", the software did not stabilise into a single programming
language in the normal sense, and remained as a continually evolving research tool
within a small community.   KRL has been superceded by **LOOPS** <131>.

Contributor: Graeme Ritchie.

Reference

[Bobrow and Winograd 77]
               Bobrow, D.G. and Winograd, T.
               An overview of KRL, a knowledge representation language.
               Cognitive Science 1, 1977.

116. LAPLACIAN

The Laplacian is the lowest (second) order circularly symmetric differential
operator.   When convolved with a 2-d function (e.g. an image) it computes the
non-directional second derivative of that function.   See also **convolution** <45>.

Contributors: T P Pridmore, S R Pollard, S T Stenton.

Reference

[Marr 82]   Marr, D.
               Vision.
               Freeman, 1982.

117. LCF

An interactive system for generating proofs in a logic which combines
predicate calculus and the **lambda calculus**.   Proof strategies are expressed in a
functional programming language **ML** <146>.   Complex strategies can be built up from
simpler ones using higher-order functions called **tacticals**.   For example:

(INDUCTION ORELSE CASES) THEN SIMPLIFY is an ML expression describing a strategy which first tries INDUCTION (a given strategy); if that fails CASES is tried, and then the resulting subgoals are passed to SIMPLIFY. The infixed binary operators ORELSE and THEN are tacticals.

Contributor: Mike Gordon.

Availability

Available as a research tool with informal support.

Environment: VAX/Unix with FranzLisp, Multics MACLISP
            DEC-10/Tops-10 with UCI or Rutgers LISP.

From: Larry Paulson (VAX/Unix)
      Computer Laboratory,
      University of Cambridge,
      Corn Exchange Street,
      Cambridge CB2 3QG.
      England.

      Electronic address: lcp%camsteve@ucl-cs

      Gerard Huet (Multics/MACLISP)
      INRIA,
      Rocquencourt,
      B.P. 105-78153,
      Le Chesnay,
      FRANCE.

      John Scott (DEC-10 versions)
      Department of Computer Science,
      Edinburgh University,
      JCMB, King's Buildings,
      Mayfield road,
      Edinburgh,
      Scotland.

Tel: (031) 667-1081

Reference

[Gordon, Milner and Wadsworth 79]
                Gordon, M. Milner, R. and Wadsworth, C.
                Lecture Notes in Computer Science. Volume 78: *Edinbrugh LCF.*
                Springer-Verlag, 1979.

118. LEARNING FROM SOLUTION PATHS

Starting with only the legal conditions on a set of **operators**, a strategy learning system can employ weak methods to search a problem space. Once a solution path has been found, it can be used to assign credit and blame to instances of these operators. If a move leads from a state on the solution path to another state on the solution path, it is labelled as a **positive instance** of the responsible operator.

However, if a move leads from a state on the solution path to a state not on the path, it is marked as a **negative instance**. These classifications can then be input to a condition-finding mechanism (such as the generalization, discrimination or **version space <256>** methods); which will determine the heuristically useful conditions under which each operator should be applied.

Contributor: Pat Langley.

Reference

[Sleeman, Langley and Mitchell 82]
           Sleeman, D., Langley, P. and Mitchell, T.M.
           Learning from solution paths: An approach to the credit assignment
             problem.
           AI Magazine , 1982.

119. LEXICAL ACCESS

Alias: dictionary lookup.

There are various techniques for accessing lexical information ranging from the sensible, e.g. the use of a tree structure on a letter-per-branch basis, to the ridiculous, e.g. linear search. The larger the lexicon the more important it becomes to relate word frequency to the access method. (In English, say, a mere 100 word types account for over 50% of the word tokens in running text.) It also becomes more important to take a general approach to the problems of inflected forms, e.g. past tenses, plurals, and spelling rules or morphographemics **<149>**.

Contributor: Henry Thompson.

References

[Kaplan and Kay 82]
           Kaplan, R.M. and Kay, M.
           Word recognition.
           Technical Report, Xerox Palo Alto Research Center, 1982.
           To appear.

[Kay 77]   Kay, M.
           Morphological and syntactic analysis.
           In Zampolli, A. (editor), *Linguistic Structures Processing*, . North
             Holland, 1977.

120. LIFER

A system developed at SRI for creating English language interfaces to other software systems, e.g. database query systems. It was designed to elicit domain- and task-referring expressions appropriate to a given application software system, and to extract from these the syntax and semantics of a grammar for an appropriately specialised natural language interface system. LIFER was intended to have sufficient power, robustness and flexibility for convenient interface building and use by persons without technical linguistic expertise, i.e. to be a contribution to human engineering for system building. Its two components, the language specification functions and the parser, essentially allowed interface bootstrapping from a quite small base. LIFER's successor is **TEAM**.

Contributor: Karen Sparck Jones.

Reference

[Hendrix 77]   Hendrix, G. G.
                The LIFER Manual
                TN 138 edition, SRI International, Menlo Park, 1977.

121. LINE FINDING

Alias: **boundary detection**.

Any computer program that detects lines in a **grey-level array <89>**.   Typically a line finder will look for discontinuities in the grey-level array and group them into connected sets.   There are many different techniques for deciding which intensity variations are significant, and for deciding on the best grouping into lines.   See also **edge detection <65>**.

Contributor: Alan Bundy.

122. LINE LABELLING

Huffmann and Clowes conceptualised the task of interpreting straight line drawings in terms of attaching labels like 'concave', 'convex', 'occluding' to lines, interpreted as depicting object edges. See **junction dictionary <110>** and **relaxation labelling <210>**.

Contributor: Aaron Sloman.

Reference

[Clowes 71]   Clowes, M. B.
               On seeing things.
               Artificial Intelligence 2, 1971.

123. LINEAR PREDICTIVE CODING

If one approximates the vocal tract as a series of fixed length tubes (which is equivalent to representing it as an all-pole digital filter) it becomes possible to predict successive samples of the speech wave as linear combinations of previous samples.   The coefficients in the linear combination characterize the shape of the vocal tract.   A sequence of sets of coefficients can be used to characterize the changing shape of the vocal tract over time.   This representation is widely used because of the particularly efficient algorithms associated with it.

Contributor: Steve Isard.

124. LISPKIT

Lispkit is a variant of full Lisp designed to support programming in a purely functional style. Its implementation is an abstract machine, which can be emulated in hardware or software, and a range of programs (compilers, editors etc.) each of which runs on the abstract machine and which together provide the program development environment for Lispkit programming. Currently Lispkit implementations are available on the Perq, the Vax, the Sirius and the Sage. The system is easily moved to new machines simply by reprogramming the abstract machine.

Contributor: Peter Henderson.

References

[Henderson 82] Henderson, P.
Functional Programming – Application and Implementation.
Prentice Hall, 1982.

[Henderson et al. 83]
Henderson, P., Jones, G and Jones, S.B.
Lispkit – manual and sources
Programming Research Group, Oxford University, 1983.
in press.

125. LM

LM is a **robot programming** <217> language at the "end-effector" level which enables the description of an assembly task to be made in terms of the motion of one or several arms, the operation of their tools and the data provided by the sensors. The world is modelled using **cartesian frames**, and frames can also be attached to objects. Arm motion can be specified in terms of these frames. In syntax LM resembles a classical programming language such as **ALGOL-60**.

Contributor: Pat Ambler.

Reference

[Latombe and Mazer 81]
Latombe, J.C. and Mazer, E.
LM: A High-Level Programming Language for Controlling Assembly Robots.
In *11th Int Symp on Industrial Robots*. , 1981.

126. LM-GEO

LM-GEO is an extension of the high level **robot programming** language **LM** <125>. It allows the programmer to give explicit positions to frames by describing geometric relationships between objects, much in the way that **RAPT** <205> does. An inference system converts descriptions in terms of spatial relationships into frames as used by the LM system.

Contributor: Pat Ambler.

Reference

[Mazer]   Mazer, E.
                LM-GEO: Geometric programming of Assembly Robots.
                Rapport de recherche 296, IMAG, Grenoble,France,

127. LOCAL GREY-LEVEL OPERATIONS

Alias: **image morphology**.

A class of transformations on **grey level images** <89> which replace each **pixel** (in parallel) by some function of its neighbouring pixels.

In pointwise operations the new pixel value is independent of the neighbourhood, for example simple grey scale remapping such as histogram equalisation.

Linear operations (**convolution** <45>) are used for filtering (local averaging etc) and feature detection (such as **edge detection** <65>).

Non-linear operations can be developed using local minimum and local maximum functions to replace summation.   Such operations can also be regarded as grey level generalisations of binary morphological operations using the **fuzzy logic** based replacement of AND by MIN and OR by MAX.   Illustrative operations are "shrink" and "expand" (also called "erode" and "dilate").   In a shrink operation a "true" pixel is changed to "false" if there is a "false" pixel in some defined neighbourhood of it. Similarly for expand.   For example, if the neighbourhoods are defined as 3x3 squares then shrink will delete all edge pixels.   See [Serra 1982] for an introduction.

Some of these types of transformations have been generalised to three dimensional binary images.

Contributor: Dave Reynolds.

Reference

[Serra 82]   Serra J.
                Image Analysis and Mathematical Morphology.
                Academic Press, 1982.

128. LOGIC MACHINE ARCHITECTURE

The Logic Machine Architecture (LMA) is a layered family of software tools designed to enable the efficient and flexible use and development of significant **theorem proving** systems.   As such it is an abstraction of the implementation details of many existing theorem proving programs.   Five layers are identified:

Layer 0 implements a few primitive abstract data types that do not exist in the host language PASCAL.

Layer 1 implements the data type "object". Operations that may be performed on an object range through **unification** <252>, substitutions, access of all objects satisfying some boolean combination of user defined properties etc. This layer provides the machinery necessary for the representation and manipulation of logical formulae and associated constructs (such as substitutions). Each object may have arbitrary properties (attributes) associated with it as well as "user variables"; a form of flag for simple properties implemented in a more efficient way than the attributes.

Layer 2 provides operations and functions for constructing inference mechanisms such as **resolution** <212> inference rules and special purpose inference mechanisms such as **subsumption** checkers etc. (Although layer 1 is general enough to support a variety of formalisms, the current release of layer 2 includes only the tools for clause-based systems.)

Layer 3 provides the facilities to configure whole theorem provers. Here systems are represented as independent processes which are managed by the interprocess communication facilities of Layer 4.

The architecture is not restricted to any specific logic. It is general enough to construct **lambda calculus, natural deduction** and **Gentzen** style systems as well as resolution based systems.

Layers 3 – 5 are not implemented, but a fairly ambitious theorem-prover based on the layer 2 tools has been included in the package.

Contributor: Lincoln Wallen.

Availability

Available on request with documentation and (some) support.

Environment: VAX/VMS, Berkeley Unix, IBM CMS (Pascal/VS)

From: E.L. Lusk,
      MCSD,
      Argonne National Lab.,
      9600 Cass Ave.,
      Argonne,
      Illinois 60439,
      USA.

      Tel: 312-972-7852
      Electronic address: lusk@anl-mcs (Arpanet)

References

[Lusk, McCune and Overbeek 82a]
                Lusk, E.L., McCune, W.W., Overbeek, R.A.
                Logic Machine Architecture: Kernel Functions.
                In Loveland (editor), *6th Conference on Automated Deduction*.
                    Springer-Verlag, 1982.
                Lecture notes in computer science No. 138.

[Lusk, McCune and Overbeek 82b]
        Lusk, E.L., McCune, W.W., Overbeek, R.A.
        Logic Machine Architecture: Inference Mechanisms.
        In Loveland (editor), *6th Conference on Automated Deduction*.
            Springer-Verlag, 1982.
        Lecture notes in computer science No. 138.

129. LOGLISP

LOGLISP is an implementation of **logic programming** within **LISP** <34> developed at Syracuse University. Essentially, it is an attempt to provide LISP users with the equivalent of **PROLOG** <196> without having to venture out of already well developed LISP environments. Unlike PROLOG implementations, which employ a backtracking process to explore alternative computations, LOGLISP carries out computations in quasi-parallel. The LOGLISP system consists of LISP with a set of logic programming primitives which are collectively refered to as LOGIC. Part of the power of LOGLISP is that LISP can invoke LOGIC and LOGIC can invoke LISP.

Contributors: Robert Corlett and Kevin Poulter.

Reference

130. LOGO

LOGO is a packaged system consisting of a programming language and its environment: a graphical module that outputs either to the screen or a "turtle". LOGO also embodies a philosophy of education. The language is essentially **LISP** <34> with extra syntactic structures. The graphics are based on **turtle geometry**, emphasising movement relative to the current position of the "turtle" rather than Cartesian geometry. The educational philosophy emphasises creative learning by the exploration of an environment.

Contributor: Robert Hawley.

Reference

[Papert 80]   Papert S.
                Mindstorms.
                Basic Books, 1980.

131. LOOPS

LOOPS (LISP OBJECT ORIENTATED PROGRAMMING SYSTEM) adds data, object, and rule orientated programming to the procedure orientated programming of Interlisp-D (<103>). In object orientated programming, behaviour is determined by responses of instances of classes to messages sent between these objects with no direct access to the internal structure of an object. Data orientated programming is a dual of object orientated programming, where behaviour can occur as a side effect of accessing data. Rule orientated programming is an alternative to programming in LISP (<34>). Programs in this paradigm are organised around recursively composable sets or pattern-action rules for use in **expert system** design. LOOPS is integrated into **Interlisp-D**, and thus provides access to the standard procedure orientated programming of Lisp, and use of the extensive environmental support of the Interlisp-D system.

Contributor: Martin Gittins.

Availability

Not currently available.

Environment: Interlisp-D on Xerox 1108 only.

From: David Catton,
Artificial Intelligence Ltd.,
62-78 Merton Rd.,
Watford WD1 7BY,
England.

Tel: 0923-47707

Reference

[Bobrow and Stefik]
Bobrow, D.G. and Stefik, M.
The LOOPS Manual

132. **MACLISP**

Major dialect of **LISP** ‹34›, distinguished by (a) use of linked text-editor for structure editing, and (b) powerful compiler requiring some type declarations in the source. Emphasis: use for systems programming.

Contributor: Bruce Anderson.

Availability

Available on request with documentation.

Environment: DEC PDP-10 or -20 or equivalent (any operating system on those machines).

From: Pandora Berman,   (Documentation): Publications Office,
Room 912,   Laboratory for C.S.,
545 Technology Square,   545 Technology Square.
Cambridge,
Mass 02139,
USA.

Reference

[Moon]   Moon, D.
                 Maclisp Reference manual
                 MIT AI Lab., .

[Moon (Revised)]
                 Moon, D.
                 Revised Maclisp Reference Manual TR – 295.
                 Pitman, .

133. MACRO OPERATORS

Alias: **MACROPS, triangle table.**

It is possible to combine a sequence of operators to build a new one, a macro operator, that has the effect of the sequence. Its list of preconditions contains all preconditions of the first operator of the sequence, plus those of later operators in so far as they have not been satisfied by previous operators in the sequence. The ADD and DELETE LISTS are determined in the same way.

Macro operators can be represented like 'basic' operators and be added to the set of existing operators. This is a form of **learning** that will reduce search in new problems.

Contributor: Maarten van Someren.

Reference

[Fikes, R.E., Hart, P.E. and Nilsson, N.J. 72]
                 Fikes, R.E., Hart, P.E. and Nilsson, N.J.
                 Learning and executing generalized robot plans.
                 Artificial Intelligence 3, 1972.

134. MACSYMA

MACSYMA is an interactive system that assists in solving mathematical problems. It can apply a wide range of mathematical transformations to symbolic inputs and can yield symbolic results, numerical results or FORTRAN programs. It can manipulate algebraic expressions, vectors, tensors, inequalities and series. The system can carry out symbolic integration, differentiation and simplification. When a problem has no algebraic solution it can resort to numerical approximations. The whole process is guided by the user. There is also an extensive plotting package.

Contributor: Robert Corlett.

Availability

Commercially available with documentation and support. Special rates for Government, non-profit organizations and academic institutions.

68

Environment: VAX running VMS or Unix, TOPS 20, Multics, Symbolics 3600,
68000 (forthcoming).

From: Dr. Richard Pavelle,
MACSYMA Product Manager,
Symbolics Incorporated,
MACSYMA Group,
257 Vassar street,
Cambridge, MA 02139,
USA.

Tel: (617) 864-4600
Electronic address: RP@MIT-MC

Reference

[MACSYMA 83]   Mathlab group.
A Brief Overview of MACSYMA
MIT Computer Science Lab., 1983.

135. MARKGRAF KARL REFUTATION PROCEDURE

Developed at the University of Karlsruhe, West Germany, the Markgraf Karl is one of the largest **theorem proving** projects undertaken. It is implemented in **INTERLISP** ‹103› and advances the thesis that theorem provers must be guided by large amounts of domain specific knowledge in order to overcome the combinatorial explosions traditionally associated with unguided theorem provers.

The system is separated into two layers: the **Supervisor** and the **Logic Engine**. The task of the Supervisor is to collect together the relevant information (axioms, definitions etc.) for the problem at hand and to decide on a suitable proof method (such as induction) engaging the necessary modules to carry this out.

The Logic Engine is based on the **connection graph resolution** ‹207› proof procedure augmented with powerful heuristics for reducing the **search space** even further, and spotting redundant inferences. A "monitor" oversees the refutation process and selects the connections on which to resolve. Only a small proportion of the connections are "active" at any given time (and hence candidates for resolution); thus the theorem prover exhibits very directed behaviour which leads to corresponding increases in efficiency. The MKRP-System is currently among the strongest theorem proving systems internationally.

Contributor: Lincoln Wallen.

Availability

Available on request with documentation and support

Environment: Interlisp. By the end of 1984 will run on KK-Lisp.
Siemens 7600, VAX, Lisp-machine.
Source code c. 2000 K (Bytes).
Min. storage required for actual run: 4000 K.

From: Joerg H. Siekmann,
        Universitat Kaiserslautern,
        Fachbeireich Informatik,
        Postfach 30 49,
        D-6750 Kaiserslautern,
        West Germany.

        Tel: 0631-205-2855

Reference

[Mark G. Raph 84]
            Raph, K. M. G.
            The Markgraf Karl Refutation Procedure.
            Memo SEKI-MK-84-01, Universitat Kaiserslautern, 1984.

136. MBASE

An **expert system** shell for **intelligent front ends**, implemented in **Prolog** <196>. MBase is a domain-independent version of **Mecho**, a program for solving Mechanics problems.   MBase is input a problem description, represented in predicate logic, and outputs a representation as a set of equations.   The domain must be described by a collection of formulae and by meta-properties of these formulae and of the predicates used in the original problem description.   The output equations are instantiations of these formulae.   MBase incorporates the **Marples   Algorithm**, a technique for extracting equations from the input representation, and various special purpose, but domain independent, inference mechanisms for bridging the gap between the knowledge in the input representation and that required by the formulae. MBase has been applied to Mechanics, Statistics and Ecology.

Contributor: Alan Bundy.

Availability

Available with documentation.

Environment: PROLOG on DEC 10 under TOPS 10. Can be adapted for other
            PROLOG systems.

From: Jane Hesketh,
        Dept. of Artificial Intelligence,
        Hope Park Square,
        University of Edinburgh,
        Edinburgh,
        Scotland.

        Tel: 031-667-1011 ext. 6831
        Electronic address: hesketh@edxa

Reference

[Bundy, Byrd and Mellish 82]
        Bundy, A., Byrd, L. and Mellish, C.
        Special Purpose, but Domain Independent Inference Mechanisms.
        In *Proceedings of ECAI-82*, pages 67-74. European Conference on
           Artificial Intelligence, 1982.
        Also available from Edinburgh as DAI Research Paper No. 179.

137 MDL

MDL is a LISP-like language in that it uses prefix notation, can treat programs as data, and can be run interpreted or compiled. MDL differs from other LISP dialects in that it supports a large number of built-in data types, has a facility for users to define data types, and has a richer syntax than LISP.

Contributor: Chris Reeve.

Availability

Available as a research tool with (some) documentation.

Environment: DEC-20/TOPS-20, VAX/Unix 4.2.

From: Chris Reeve,
     MIT Lab. for Computer Science,
     NE43 - 218A,
     545 Technology Square,
     Cambridge ,
     Mass 02139,
     USA.

     Tel: (617) 253-1428
     Electronic address: clr@mit-xx

138. MEANS/ENDS ANALYSIS

A technique for controlling search. Given a current state and a goal state, an operator is chosen which will reduce the difference between the two. This operator is applied to the current state to produce a new state, and the process is recursively applied to this new state and the goal state.

Contributor: Alan Bundy.

Reference

[Newell and Simon 63]
        Newell, A. and Simon, H.A.
        GPS, a program that simulates human thought.
        In Feigenbaum, E. and Feldman,F. (editor), *Computers and
           Thought*, pages 279-293. McGrawHill, 1963.

139. META-LEVEL INFERENCE

The prefix **meta-** (contrast **object-**) denotes a language whose subject matter is the <u>representation</u> of some theory, as distinct from the theory itself.   Thus

- $x^2 - 3x + 2 = 0 \Rightarrow x = 1$ or 2.

- $x^2 - 3x + 2 = 0$ contains two occurrences of the unknown 'x',

are statements in respectively the theory and the meta-theory of algebra.

Meta-level inference denotes the use of meta-level expressions to control or guide the application of object-level knowledge-sources (rewrite rules, axioms, production rules, etc.)

Use of the term implies that the meta- and object-languages are clearly distinguished: however, the functional relationship between the two may take a number of forms.   The possible variety is illustrated by the following examples.

The program PRESS [Sterling et al 82], which solves symbolic equations, is written entirely at the meta-level (in PROLOG (<196>)).   Clauses which represent meta-algebraic procedures (such as 'collect', which reduces the number of occurrences of the unknown) are defined in terms of the rewrite rules which carry out these procedures.   Hence resolutions between clauses effect the application of rewrite rules to the given equation.   The application of procedures is controlled by **precondition analysis** <186>.   Thus M-L.I. is used to transform an object-level **search** into a meta-level search with much lower branching rate, and where most branches lead to solutions.   Furthermore, its expressive power is needed to state the preconditions.

In Davis' program, the meta-rules give information about the utility of object-rules.   The control sequence is

1. Select rules and meta-rules relevant to the given problem.

2. Apply the meta-rules to re-order and/or prune the list of rules.

3. Execute the modified list of rules.

Thus, the program is object-driven, and the meta-rules re-order or prune the branches of the object-level search tree.

In FOL, a simplification algorithm is constructed in which object and meta-rules are applied in turn.   Also, meta-knowledge may be 'reflected' into the object-level: instantiated, and applied to algebraic objects.

In contrast with the above, MOLGEN has three levels.   The object level contains knowledge about genetics, the second level, knowledge about planning experiments, and the top level, knowledge about strategy (choosing between heuristic and least-commitment).   Each level controls steps in the level below.   (See also <140>.)

Contributor: Robin Boswell

References

[Aiello and Weyrauch 80]
Aiello, L. and Weyrauch, R. W.
Using Meta-Theoretic Reasoning to do Algebra.
In Bibel, W. and Kowalski, R. (editors), *5th Conference on Automated Deduction*, pages 1-13. Springer Verlag, 1980.
Lecture Notes in Computer Science No. 87.

[Davis 80]
Davis, R.
Meta-Rules: Reasoning about Control.
Artificial Intelligence 15: 179-222, 1980.

[Stefik 81]
Stefik, M.
Planning and Meta-planning (MOLGEN: Part 2).
Artificial Intelligence 16: 141-170, 1981.

[Sterling et al 82]
Sterling, L., Bundy, A., Byrd, L., O'Keefe, R., and Silver, B.
Solving Symbolic Equations with PRESS.
In Calmet, J. (editor), *Computer Algebra, Lecture Notes in Computer Science No. 144.*, pages 109-116. Springer Verlag, 1982.
Longer version available from Edinburgh as Research Paper 171.

140. META-PLANNING

Meta-planning is a technique whereby the operations carried out upon a plan as it is created eg forward and backward extension, **top-down** elaboration, **constraint propagation** <39>, are themselves regarded as actions to be planned at a **meta-level**. The technique provides great control flexibility compared with systematic elaboration techniques or **agendas**.

Contributor: Jim Doran.

Reference

[Stefik 80]
Stefik, M. J.
Planning and Meta-Planning (Molgen: part 2).
Artificial Intelligence 14, 1980.

141. META-RULES

In the context of linguistics, meta-rules are a way of increasing the expressive power of a grammatical formalism. Informally, a grammar with meta-rules added provides two ways of including rules in a grammar - explicitly, by adding individual rules, or implicitly, by adding meta-rules. A meta-rule says 'If there is a rule of such-and-such a form in the grammar, then take the grammar as also containing another rule of such-and-such a form'.

Context-free grammars <41> are well suited to extension by meta-rule.

Contributor: Henry Thompson.

References

[Gazdar 81]   Gazdar, G.
               Phrase Structure Grammar.
               In Jacobson and Pullum (editor), *The Nature of Syntactic Representations*. Reidel, Dordrecht, 1981.

[Thompson 82] Thompson, H.S.
               Handling Metarules in a Parser for GPSG.
               In Barlow, M., Flickinger, D. and Sag, I. (editor), *Developments in Generalised Phrase Structure Grammar*. Bloomington, Indiana University Linguistics Club, 1982.
               Stanford Working Papers in Grammatical Theory Volume 2.

142. MICRO EXPERT

A **Bayesian inference expert system**, shell similar to the **Prospector** inference engine.   It supports a number of data input schemes and makes some use of **semantic nets** <227>.   Operates by a compile stage and a run-time interpreter. Available for a number of micros – on a commercial footing in the UK, and is written in **PASCAL**.

Contributor: John Lumley.

Availability

Commercially available with documentation.

From: Isis Systems Ltd.,
      11 Oakdene Road,
      Redhill,
      Surrey RH1 6BT,
      England.

Reference

[Cox 83]   Cox, P.
               Micro Expert Reference Manual
               Isis Systems Ltd., 1983.

143. MICRO-PLANNER

PLANNER was an early AI programming language developed by Hewitt at MIT in the early seventies.   A subset of the language, **Micro-PLANNER**, was implemented by Sussman, Winograd and Charniak in **MACLISP** <132>.   A PLANNER system embedded in **POP-2** <181> was implemented as POPLER.   Programs consist of theorems (statements about how to achieve certain types of goals i.e.   procedural knowledge) and assertions (statements expressing facts about the problem domain). The invocation of theorems (procedures) is **pattern directed** (see <173>) and the semantics of the language is based on that of a **theorem prover**.

Theorems come in two flavours **"consequent"** and **"antecedent"**.   The consequent theorems are invoked when a goal matches the pattern of the theorem; thus the theorem embodies the procedural knowledge of which goals it may be used to solve. An antecedent theorem is invoked when an assertion that matches its pattern is added to or removed from the global database. They are mainly used to implement **demons** <51>. Micro-PLANNER uses a rigid **depth-first search** <55> regime with **chronological backtracking** to search the space for possible solution.

PLANNER was criticized for its rigid backtracking control structure and the lack of control primitives available for use by the programmer. (See **CONNIVER** <38>). However the ideas on **pattern matching** <174> and **associative databases** have survived and are major features of many contemporary AI languages such as **PROLOG** <196>.

Contributor: Lincoln Wallen.

Reference

[Sussman et al. 71]
Sussman, G. J., Winograd, T., and Charniak, E.
Micro-PLANNER reference manual
AI Laboratory, MIT, 1971.
AI Memo 203A.

144. MICRO-PROLOG

A dialect of **PROLOG** <196> specifically developed for microcomputers. It includes a tracing package, a structure editor, and a front end called **Simple** which presents the PROLOG facilities in a particularly easy-to-understand form. Micro-PROLOG has been used, amongst other things, for building expert system shells (e.g. **APES** <11>) and for teaching school-children logic and computing.

Contributor: Martin Merry.

Availability

Commercially available with documentation.

Environment: Z80 micros under CP/M80, 8088/8086 micros under MSDOS or CP/M86.

From: Logic Programming Associates Ltd.,
10 Burntwood Close,
London SW18 3JU,
England.

Tel: 01-874-0350

Reference

[Clark and McCabe 84]
Clark, K.L., and McCabe, F.G.
Micro-Prolog: Programming in Logic.
Prentice-Hall International, 1984.

145. MINIMAX

This is a technique for searching **game trees** in order to determine the best move in a given position. The limited lookahead gametree is used and the values of the leaves are given. Minimax starts from the leaves and works up to the root of the tree. If MAX is to play at a node, the minimum possible value at that node is taken to be the the nodes value. In this way MAX maximizes his/her gain, assuming optimal play by the opponent. Working up from the leaves the values of the possible moves in the initial state are calculated.

Contributor: Maarten van Someren.

Reference

146. ML

ML is the metalanguage of the **LCF** <117> system. It is a fully **higher-order**, functional programming language supporting **polymorphic types**, designed for writing **theorem proving** strategies. Implementations in **LISP** and **PASCAL** exist for a variety of machines (DEC10, VAX, Honeywell).

Contributor: Mike Gordon.

Availability

Available as a research tool with informal support as part of the LCF system only. See **LCF** <117> for distribution details.

Reference

[Gordon 82]   Gordon, M.J.C.
                Representing a Logic in the LCF Metalanguage.
                In D. Neel (editor), *Tools and Notions for Program Construction,* .
                Cambridge University Press, 1982.

147. MODEL DIRECTED SEARCH

Alias: **generate and test**.

Problem solving can be viewed as the process of generating solutions from observed or given data. Unfortunately, it is not always possible to use direct methods (i.e. go from data to solution directly), instead, we often have to use indirect or model-based methods. If we have a model of the real world we can test the results we would expect from hypothetical solutions against those that we desire or observe in the real world.

The model directed search technique is to generate some plausible solutions from some initial conditions and test them using the model. If necessary, we return to the generate stage, forming more solutions in the light of our test results then test these. This is repeated until an acceptable solution is found.

Examples of systems using model directed search are **Meta-Dendral** and **Casnet**.

Contributor: Robert Corlett.

References

[Feigenbaum et al 71]
    Feigenbaum, E.A., Buchanan, B.G., and Lederberg, J.
    On Generality and Problem Solving: a Case Study Using the
     DENDRAL Program.
    In *Machine Intelligence 6*, . Edinburgh University Press, 1971.

[Weiss et al 78] Weiss, S.M., Kulikowski, C.A., Amarel, S., and Safir, A.
    A Model Based Method for Computer-Aided Medical Decision Making.
    Artificial Intelligence , 1978.

148. MODULATION TRANSFER FUNCTION

Modulation transfer function is a description of a system's frequency response. It is a plot of the input to output amplitude ratio as a function of the frequency of the sinusoidally modulated input signal.

Contributor: Jon Mayhew.

Reference

[Campbell and Robson 68]
    Campbell, F.W.C. and Robson, J.
    Application of fourier analysis to the visibility of gratings.
    J. Physiol. (Lond) 197: 551-566, 1968.

149. MORPHOGRAPHEMICS

Alias: spelling rules.

The productivity of word-formation processes in many languages make it impossible to have every word in the lexicon. Systematic characterisation of the regularities in computationally exploitable fashion is the concern of computational morphographemics. The characterisation has to cover both combination and respelling constraints on word components. Simple ad hoc approaches to segmenting words so that their components can be looked up in the dictionary are fairly easy to devise for languages like English.

Contributor: Henry Thompson.

References

[Kaplan and Kay 82]
Kaplan, R.M. and Kay, M.
Word recognition.
Technical Report, Xerox Palo Alto Research Center, 1982.
To appear.

[Kay 77]
Kay, M.
Morphological and syntactic analysis.
In Zampolli, A. (editor), *Linguistic Structures Processing*, . North
Holland, 1977.

[Koskenniemi 83] Koskenniemi, K.
Two-Level Model for Morphological Analysis.
In Bundy, A. (editor), *Proceedings of the Eighth International Joint
Conference on Artificial Intelligence*. International Joint
Conference on Artificial Intelligence, W. Kaufmann, Los Altos,
CA, 1983.

150. MPROLOG

MProlog is an efficient, modular **Prolog** <196> system supporting both the
development phase of programming and efficiency tuning for production programs.
Its components are:

- the pretranslator, for converting MProlog modules into an efficiently
  executable internal form;

- the consolidator, for linking separately pretranslated modules into a
  program;

- the interpreter, for interpretation of a consolidated program;

- the Program Development Subsystem (PDSS), which provides a user-
  friendly environment for interactive development of MProlog modules.

MProlog was developed by the Institute for Coordination of Computer Techniques
(SZKI), 1054 Budapest, Akademia u. 17, Hungary.

Contributor: Steve Todd.

Availability

From: Dr. Julia Sipka,
       SCIL-Systems,
       Computers and Informatics Laboratory,
       1011 Budapest,
       Iskola u.10,
       HUNGARY.

References

[Bendl, Koves and Szeredi 80]
> Bendl, J., Koves, P., and Szeredi, P.
> *The MProlog System*
> 1980.
> Logic Programming Workshop, Debrecen, Hungary.

[Szeredi and Santane-Toth 82]
> Szeredi, P. and Santane-Toth, E.
> Prolog Applications in Hungary.
> In Clark, K. and Tarnlund, S-A. (editor), *Logic Programming*.
> 1982.

151. MULTI-ACTOR SYSTEM

Alias: **multi-agent system**.

A multi-actor system is a combination of two or more **plan generation** and **plan execution** systems (**actors**) which act and intercommunicate in a shared task environment.

Communication actions between actors (eg request for information, provision of information, provision of partial plan) may be handled as ordinary actions and are closely related to **speech acts** in natural language theory.

Techniques have been devised whereby one actor's beliefs about the beliefs of another may be expressed and computed.

Note: this use of the term "actor" is substantially different from that employed in the actor model of computation (see **actors <4>**).

Contributor: Jim Doran.

References

[Thorndyke, McArthur and Cammarata 81]
> Thorndyke, P.W., McArthur D. and Cammarata, S.
> AUTOPILOT: a distributed planner for airfleet control.
> In *Proceedings of IJCAI-81*. International Joint Conference on
> Artificial Intelligence, 1981.

[Wilks and Bien]
> Wilks Y. and Bien J.
> Beliefs, point of view and multiple environments.
> *Cognitive Science* , .

152. MULTI-PULSE LPC

Alias: **modified linear predictive analysis, synthesis of speech, vocoder**.

An improved technique of **linear predictive coding** <123> in which the normal white noise or impulses excitation of the **linear predictive filter** is replaced by a modified impulse excitation only.   A **perceptually weighted spectrum matching** technique is used to place the impulses.

Contributor: Andrew Varga.

Reference

[Atal and Remde 82]
        Atal, B.S. and Remde,J.R.
        A new model of LPC excitation for producing natural sounding speech
          at low bit rates.
        In *Proc. IEEE ICASSP*, pages 614-617.   1982.

153. NATURAL DEDUCTION

Natural deduction is a formal inference system which is said naturally to mirror the way in which humans reason.   A natural deduction system consists of rules of inference eliminating and introducing each of the connectives and quantifiers of the predicate calculus.   There are twelve rules which may be used to infer conclusions. Two examples of such rules are given below:

$$
\begin{array}{cc}
 & \begin{array}{c} \underline{\quad\quad}\ i \\ A \\ \vdots \\ B \end{array} \\
\begin{array}{c} A \qquad A \to B \\ \hline \quad\quad B \end{array} & \begin{array}{c} \overline{\quad\quad\quad}i \\ A \to B \end{array}
\end{array}
$$

The rule on the left is that to eliminate the $\to$ connective and that on the right to introduce it.

Natural deduction proofs are trees, the leaves representing the assumptions, and the root, the conclusion that has been deduced from those assumptions.   It is valid in natural deduction to assume temporarily certain formulae, and then 'discharge' these assumptions later in the proof, by using certain of the deduction rules.   The $\to$ Introduction rule above is an example of a rule which discharges an assumption, namely A in this case.   Natural deduction is sound and complete.

The UT Theorem Prover <254> of Bledsoe et al uses a natural deduction system because it is intended to be interactive, and is thus required to proceed in a manner natural to humans.

Contributor: Dave Plummer.

Reference

[Tennant 78]   Tennant, N.
               Natural Logic.
               Edinburgh University Press, Edinburgh, 1978.

154. NEGATION AS FAILURE

Negation as failure is a **rule of inference** which allows one to deduce that NOT P is true if all possible proofs of P fail.

This is the way that negation is treated in **PROLOG** <196> and **Micro-PLANNER** <143>. When using a system for database access, the assumption that negation as failure corresponds to true negation is precisely a consequence of the **Closed World Assumption** i. e. the assumption that all relevant information is contained in the database. Without the Closed World Assumption, negation as failure corresponds to "we assume something is false if we cannot deduce it from available information", which is not the same as true negation.

Contributor: Martin Merry.

References

[Clark 78]   Clark, K. L.
Negation as failure.
In Gallaire, H. and Minker, J. (editor), *Logic and DataBases*,
      pages 293-322. Plenum Press, 1978.

[Reiter 78]   Reiter, R.
On Closed World DataBases.
In Gallaire, H. and Minker, J. (editor), *Logic and DataBases*,
      pages 55-76. Plenum Press, 1978.

155. NEIGHBOURHOOD PARALLELISM

The technique of using immediate parallel access to the whole set of locations that form the neighbourhood of an operation. This may be restricted to a single bit plane. See **cellular arrays** <29>.

Contributors: T P Pridmore, S R Pollard, S T Stenton.

Reference

[Danielsson and Levialdi 81]
Danielsson, P. and Levialdi, S.
Computer Architectures for Pictorial Information Systems.
IEEE Computer : 53-67, November, 1981.

156. NIAL (NESTED INTERACTIVE ARRAY LANGUAGE)

A programming language based on array theory, combining **APL** and **LISP** programming concepts. All data objects in NIAL are arrays, with truth values, integers, reals, complex numbers, characters, phrases and faults as atomic arrays. Operations are built on a small core of primitive operations. The effect of applying operations is displayed as diagrams which depict shape and contents of arrays.

Contributor: Janet Efstathiou.

Availability

Commercially available with documentation and support. Special rates to academic institutions.

Environment: VAX–Unix, VAX–VMS, IBM 4341 VM–CMS, IBM PC MS DOS, or any 68000 or NS 16032 based micro running Unix with at least 512K bytes.

From: Brunel and QMC (development versions) or

Bill Jenkins,
Nial Systems Ltd.,
20 Hatter St.,
Kingston,
Ontario,
Canada K7M 2L5.

Tel: (613) 549–1432

References

[Adams 82]   W.S. Adams.
                Plain Programming in NIAL.
                Technical Report, Computing and Information Science, Queens
                    University, Kingston, Canada, June, 1982.

[Queen's University 83a]
                M.A. Jenkins.
                Q'Nial Reference Manual
                Nial Systems Limited, 1983.

[Queen's University 83b]
                L. Sutherland.
                Q'Nial Users Guide
                Nial Systems Limited, 1983.

[Schmidt and Jenkins 82]
                Fl. Schmidt and M.A. Jenkins.
                Data Systems Design and the Nial Approach.
                Technical Report, Computing and Information Science, Queens
                    University, Kingston, Canada, June, 1982.

157. NIL

NIL is a Lisp dialect under development at MIT, which runs on the VAX under VMS. NIL is a superset of Common Lisp, and contains most of the special Maclisp extensions (e.g. defstruct), and a version of the Flavours system allowing object-oriented programming.

Contributor: Kevin Poulter.

Availability

Available with documentation. Informally supported; updates supplied on request.

Environment: VAX-VMS. 12 to 25 megabytes of disk storage, depending on
whether sources are kept online. Recommended minimum of one
megabyte available memory per user plus sufficient virtual
memory – approximately 10 megabytes to a user's paging file.

From: Glenn S. Burke,
MIT Lab for Computer Science,
545 Technology Square,
Cambridge MA 02139, USA.

Tel: (617) 253-3546
Electronic address: GSB@MIT-MC.ARPA

Reference

[Burke and Carrett 83]
Burke, G., and Carrett, G.
NIL Notes for Release O, Revision 1.
Technical Report, MIT, January, 1983.

158. NON-LINEAR PLANNING

Non-linear planners are able to maintain the emerging plan as a
partially- ordered network of actions. Unnecessary ordering (or linearisation) of the
actions is avoided. Only when there are conflicts between parallel branches of the
plan (such as the inability to determine the answer to a query) is an ordering
imposed. The first such system was Sacerdoti's **NOAH**.

A complete treatment of the handling of alternatives and all legal linearisations
after an interaction between **subgoals <243>** is detected was included in Tate's
NONLIN. The ability to use the same technique in the presence of time constraints
on particular actions was a feature of Vere's **DEVISER**. Most non-linear planners
also use **hierarchical planning** techniques.

Contributor: Austin Tate.

References

[Sacerdoti 77]   Sacerdoti, E. D.
A structure for plans and behaviour.
Elsevier North-Holland, New York, 1977.

[Tate 77]   Tate, A.
Generating Project Networks.
In *Proceedings of IJCAI-77*. International Joint Conference on
Artificial Intelligence, 1977.

[Vere 83]   Vere, S.A.
Planning in time = Windows and durations for activities and goals.
IEEE Trans. on Pattern Analysis and Machine Intelligence , 1983.

159. NON-MONOTONIC REASONING

Alias: **non-monotonic logic, default reasoning, truth maintenance.**

Non-monotonic logics deal with non-monotonic reasoning, that involves adopting assumptions that may have to be abandoned in the light of new information. This reasoning is called non-monotonic in contrast with the monotonicity of deductive logic, in which the addition of new axioms to a set of axioms can never decrease the set of theorems or facts; quite often the new axioms give rise to new theorems so that the set of theorems grows monotonically with the set of axioms. In non-monotonic logics, the set of theorems may lose members as well as gain members when new axioms are added.

Non-monotonicity is a common feature of ordinary reasoning. For instance, if we are told that Tweety is a bird we assume (s)he can fly, but withdraw this when we are told that (s)he is a penguin.

Contributor: Luis Jenkins.

Reference

[AI Journal 81]
Special Issue on Non-Monotonic Logic.
Journal of Artificial Intelligence Vol. 13.

160. NUMERICALLY-CONTROLLED MACHINE TOOLS

A machine tool is a power-driven machine for cutting, grinding, drilling, or otherwise shaping a metal workpiece. A numerically-controlled (NC) machine tool is a system in which actions are controlled by numerical data given by a program. The program can position a tool point in three dimensions relative to a workpiece, and can control other function such as speed, coolant flow, gaging, and selection of tools. Most NC tools can be programmed in the **APT** language with FORTRAN subroutines. The capability to perform 3D geometrical calculations makes it possible to sculpt arbitrarily complicated shapes. **Sensory feedback <229>** is used to report differences between actual and desired tool movements, and between actual and desired workpiece dimensions to cause the NC tool to correct or minimise the error. This can automatically compensate for tool wear and detect tool breakage. Robot manipulators can be used to feed blank workpieces and to remove finished ones.

Contributor: W.F. Clocksin.

References

[Faux and Pratt 79]
        Faux, I.D. and Pratt, M.J.
        Computational Geometry for Design and Manufacture.
        Ellis Horwood, 1979.

[Simon 78]   Simon, W.
        The Numerical Control of Machine Tools.
        Edward Arnold, 1978.

161. OBJECT-CENTRED CO-ORDINATES

An object is described in object-centred co-ordinates if some point on the object forms the origin of a co-ordinate system, with axes defined by the structure of the object, and all other object points are defined relative to that origin. This description is, then, independent of viewpoint. One task of a vision system is to move from **viewer-centered description** <257> to object-centered description.

Contributors: T P Pridmore, S R Pollard, S P Stenton.

Reference

[Marr 82]   Marr, D.
        Vision.
        Freeman, 1982.

162. ONE-THEN-BEST BACKTRACKING

Since there is often good local information available to indicate the prefered solution path, it is often best to try out that indicated by heuristic information before considering the many alternatives that may be available should the local choice prove faulty. Taken to the extreme, depth-first search gives something of the flavour of such a search strategy. However, gradual wandering from a valid solution path could entail backtracking through many levels when a failure is detected.

An alternative is to focus on the choice currently being made and try to select one of the local choices which seems most promising. This continues while all is going well (perhaps with some cut-off points to take a long, hard look at how well things are going). However, if a failure occurs, the whole set of alternatives which have been generated (and ranked by a heuristic evaluator) are reconsidered to select a re-focussing point for the search. Such a search strategy is used in Tate's NONLIN, for example.

Contributor: Austin Tate.

Reference

[Tate 75]   Tate, A.
        Project Planning using a Hierarchic Non-linear Planner.
        Research Report 25, Department of Artificial Intelligence, Edinburgh
           University, 1975.

163. OPERATOR TABLE

Alias: **triangle table, MACROPS.**

When **macro operators** <133> are built from elementary **operators**, the original operators and the macro operator are available, but not any subsequences of the macro operator. Eg. If O(20) was built from O(1) through O(10), then it is not possible to use the subsequence O(8) through O(10). The following representation was devised to overcome this inefficiency:

Preconditions	operator O1			
O1's PRECOND	O1's ADD LIST	operator O2		
O2's PRECOND, not in this row	facts in cell above minus DELETE O2	O2's ADD LIST	operator O3	
O3's PRECOND, not in this row	facts in cell above minus DELETE O3	facts in cell above minus DELETE O3	O3's ADD LIST	

Facts that are preconditions for an operator are marked in each cell. To reach a goal state, the program looks for a row in the table that contains the facts of the goal state. The operator of the row above is the last operator to be applied. Next, it moves back until an operator is found for which all preconditions are currently true. This is the first operator to be applied.

A triangular table like the one above may be produced as a result of a solution process. This will reduce search on future problems. The macro operators should be generalized (with respect to variable bindings) if they are to be of any use.

Contributor: Maarten van Someren.

Reference

[Fikes, Hart and Nilsson 72]
Fikes, R.E., Hart, P.E., Nilsson, N.J.
Learning and executing generalized robot plans.
Artificial Intelligence 3, 1972.

164. OPERATORS

Alias: **operator tables**.

In the context of planning, **operators** represent the (generic) actions which the actor can execute in the planning environment. Operators are commonly represented as three lists: a list of preconditions, a list of facts that will be true after application of the operator (ADD LIST) and a list of facts that will no longer be true after the operator is applied (DELETE LIST). These lists normally involve variables which must be bound for any particular instance of the action.

The difficulty encountered in fully capturing the effects of actions in non-trivial planning domains using such operators is an aspect of the **frame problem**.

Contributors: Maarten van Someren and Jim Doran.

Reference

[Nilsson 80]   Nilsson, N.J.
                Principles of Artificial Intelligence.
                Tioga Pub. Co., 1980.

165. OPPORTUNISTIC SEARCH

Some systems do not have a fixed (goal-driven (<**86**>) or data-driven) directional approach to solving a problem.   Instead a current "focus" for the search is identified on the basis of the most constrained way forwards.   This may be suggested by comparison of the current goals with the initial world model state, by consideration of the number of likely outcomes of making a selection, by the degree to which goals are instantiated, etc.   Any problem-solving component may summarise its requirements for the solution as constraints on possible solutions or restrictions of the values of variables representing objects being manipulated.   It can then suspend its operations until further information becomes available on which a more definite choice can be made.

Many such systems operate with a "blackboard" (<**19**>) through which the various components can communicate via constraint information.   The scheduling of the various tasks associated with arriving at a solution may also be dealt with through the blackboard.

Contributor: Austin Tate.

References

[Hayes 75]   Hayes, P.J.
                A Representation for Robot Plans.
                In *Proceedings of the Eighth International Joint Conference on
                    Artificial Intelligence.*   International Joint Conference on Artificial
                    Intelligence, 1975.

[Hayes-Roth and Hayes-Roth 79]
                Hayes-Roth, B. and Hayes-Roth, F.
                A Cognitive Model of Planning.
                Cognitive Science : 275-310, 1979.

[Stallman and Sussman 77]
                Stallman, R.M. and Sussman, G.J.
                Forward-Reasoning and Dependency-Directed Backtracking.
                A.I. Journal 9: 135-196, 1977.

166. OPS5

A rule-based programming language designed to build **expert systems** ; versions in **BLISS-10** and **FranzLisp** have been written. It has been used to write R1, an expert system for configuring VAX computers. Data is represented as vectors or objects with associated attribute-value pairs, and procedural knowledge takes the form of rules. Control is governed by a recognize-act cycle and the rules are antecedent-driven. OPS5 does not have a sophisticated front-end for user interaction but has a powerful **pattern-matcher** <174>. See also **production rules** <192>.

References

[Forgy and McDermott 80]
Forgy, C.L. and McDermott, J.
The OPS5 User's Manual
Carnegie-Mellon University, Department of Computer Science, 1980.
Technical Report.

[Waterman and Hayes-Roth 82]
Waterman, D. and Hayes-Roth, F.
An Investigation of Tools for Building Expert Systems.
Technical Report R-2818-NSF, Rand Corporation, June, 1982.

167. OPTICAL FLOW

The instantaneous positional velocity field, a retinal velocity map. Mathematical analysis has shown that from a monocular view of a rigid, textured, curved surface it is possible to determine the gradient of the surface at any point and the motion relative to that surface from the velocity field of the changing retinal image and its first and second spatial derivatives. See **intrinsic images** <105>.

Contributors: T P Pridmore, S R Pollard, S T Stenton.

Reference

[Longuet-Higgens and Prazdny 80]
Longuet-Higgens, H.C. and Prazdny, K.
The Interpretation of Moving Retinal Images.
Proc. R. Soc. London B208:385-387, 1980.

168. OPTIMISTIC PLAN EXECUTION

Alias: **Planex**.

When a **plan structure** <180> is executed, there is no guarantee that the sequence of planning environment states predicted by the plan will actually occur. Deviation from expectation due to faulty planning or faulty **operator** <164> execution is very likely.

When an optimistic plan execution technique executes an operator in a plan and so encounters a new environment state, it attempts to identify the new state by matching it successively against all the states predicted in the plan, working backwards from the goal. The first match found determines which operator in the plan is to be executed next. If no match is found, then replanning is needed.

The advantage of this somewhat laborious technique is that the execution of unnecessary operators may be avoided and some execution failures can be overcome by repeating the execution of operators.

Contributor: Jim Doran.

Reference

[Fikes, Hart and Nilsson 72]
> Fikes, R.E., Hart, P.E. and Nilsson, N.J.
> Learning and Executing Generalised Robot Plans.
> *Artificial Intelligence* , 1972.

169. OVERLOADED OPERATORS

Overloading is a term used to refer to the use of the same name to refer to operations on different types of data. For example the operation + is overloaded in most programming languages to mean both addition of integers and reals. Overloading allows familiar symbols to be used and reduces verbosity, although program transformation is expedited if the usual algebraic laws associated with a symbol are preserved when it is overloaded. Thus + and * should be used over a ring rather than a lattice.

Contributor: Robin Popplestone.

170. PARAMODULATION

A **rule of inference** of **predicate calculus** <189>, used to deduce a new formula from two old ones. It is used in **automatic theorem proving**, in conjunction with **resolution** <212>, as an alternative to the axioms of equality. All the three formulae involved must be in **clausal form** <33>. If $C[t']$ and D are **clauses**, where $C[t']$ indicates that C contains a particular occurrence of t'. then the rule is

```
C[t']
D v s=t          (or D v t=s)
-------
(C[s] v D)σ
```

where σ is the most general **unifier** of t and t', and is obtained by **unification** <252>. C[s] indicates that only the particular occurrence of t' is replaced by s in C, other occurrences of t' are untouched.

Contributor: Alan Bundy.

Reference

[Chang and Lee 73]
>>>
Chang, C. and Lee, R.C.
Symbolic Logic and Mechanical Theorem Proving.
Academic Press, 1973.

171. PARTIAL EVALUATION

A technique for simplifying a piece of program or generating an optimised or equivalent version in another representation. The program is represented as a set of clauses referencing tokens which stand for unknown data items. Some of the tokens are replaced by values. The clauses are run through an interpreter which produces fewer clauses with references to evaluated data items. The interpreter needs some form of closure operation or **data-directed control <47>** to ensure it does maximum evaluation.

Contributor: P.M.D. Gray.

Reference

[Elcock et al 71]
Elcock et al.
Abset: A Programming language based on sets.
In Meltzer and Michie (editor), *Machine Intelligence 6*, pages 471.
Edinburgh University Press, 1971.

172. PARTITIONED SEMANTIC NET

Alias: partitioned semantic network.

Means of enhancing the organisational and expressive power of **semantic nets<227>** through the grouping of nodes and links, associated with Hendrix. Nodes and links may figure in one or more 'spaces', which may themselves be bundled into higher-level 'vistas', which can be exploited autonomously and structured hierarchically. The effective encoding of logical statements involving **connectives** and **quantifiers** was an important motivation for partitioning, but the partitioning mechanisms involved are sufficiently well-founded, general and powerful to support the dynamic representation of a wide range of language and world knowledge; and partitioned nets have been extensively used for a range of such purposes at SRI.

Contributor: Karen Sparck Jones.

Reference

[Hendrix 79]
Hendrix, G.G.
Encoding Knowledge in Partitioned Networks.
In Findler, N.V. (editor), *Associative Networks*, . AcademicPress, 1979.

173. PATTERN DIRECTED RETRIEVAL/INVOCATION

The retrieval of a datum from a **database** by virtue of its syntactic form. A **pattern** (or template) of the required datum is compared with the data in the database; data that "match" with the pattern are retrieved. A successful match may bind the unspecified parts (variables) of either or both of the pattern and "target" datum. In the case of procedure invocation, a pattern is associated with each procedure. Calls to a procedure are made when the current situation or goal matches the associated pattern of the procedure. This allows for a more flexible control flow as procedures are not called by name but by content. This form of retrieval/invocation is central to the **PLANNER** <143> type languages; two way **pattern matching** <174> (or **unification** <252>) being the basis of the resolution principle on which **PROLOG** <196> is based.

Contributor: Lincoln Wallen.

<u>Reference</u>

[Waterman and Hayes-Roth 78]
　　　　　Waterman, D.A., and Hayes-Roth, F. (eds.).
　　　　　Pattern directed inference systems.
　　　　　Academic Press, New York, 1978.

174. PATTERN MATCHING

In its most general form a pervasive feature of, or basis for, AI systems: the essential objective is to test whether a specific received data structure is an instance of a given general pattern, and particularly, to establish whether input data items can provide values for **pattern variables**. The matching can be made more or less fuzzy, according to the conditions on the individual pattern variables, and on their joint satisfaction. Pattern matching is important in AI because it reflects (a) the fact that complex general concepts exhibit considerable variation in particular manifestations, and (b) the fact that individual elements of these participate in relationships with one another.

Contributor: Karen Sparck Jones.

175. PERCEPTRONS

A parallel decision making mechanism that superficially resembles the sort of processing that may be characteristic of neurones in the brain. It is a pattern recognition device with a threshold. If the linear combination of the 'weighted inputs' is greater than some threshold value then the perceptron 'fires'. It is possible for a perceptron to learn, eg, if the weights associated with the inputs that were active in the case of a false alarm are decreased, and weights associated with inputs that were active in the case of a miss are increased then it is intuitively plausible that recognition performance will improve; and there is a theorem that says that a perceptron will learn to recognise a class correctly over a finite number of errors. The analysis of the mathematical properties of perceptrons revealed profound limitations to their competence. These limitations are largely due to the difficulties inherent in making global decisions on the basis of only local evidence. Thus a perceptron can't tell whether a figure is connected or not, or whether there is one, and only one, instance of a pattern present. Nevertheless there is a resurgence of interest in perceptrons associated with the development of **connectionist schemes** for visual processing.

Contributor: Jon Mayhew.

176. PHOTOMETRIC STEREO

A technique for recovering shape information from reflectance maps. Given an image and a reflectance map for one light source, the intensity at a particular image location constrains the surface orientation to lie on a contour in the reflectance map. If three images are taken with different light source positions the surface orientation must lie on a known contour in each of the three associated reflectance maps, hence the intersection of these contours specifies the surface orientation.

Contributors: T P Pridmore, S R Pollard, S T Stenton.

Reference

[Marr 82]   Marr, D.
                 Vision.
                 Freeman, 1982.

177. PIPELINING

An architecture suitable for repeating the same series of operations on different data in an operator parallel fashion. The data stream flows through the pipeline of operations, each data item being at a different stage of serial processing. The operations take place in parallel, their results being passed on to the next operation. Computational efficiency is equivalent to that of performing the whole task at the rate of the most complex sub-operation. Thus the more complex and partitioned the task the more suitable it is for pipelining.

Contributors: T P Pridmore, S R Pollard, S T Stenton.

Reference

[Danielsson and Levialdi 81]
                 Danielsson, P. and Levialdi, S.
                 Computer Architectures for Pictorial Information Systems.
                 IEE Computer : 53-67, November, 1981.

178. PITCH EXTRACTION

Alias: Pitch extraction for speech synthesis and recognition.

Three programs are provided to implement the following methods of pitch extraction: Gold-Rabiner parallel processing method with voiced-unvoiced decision, Dubnowski autocorrelation method and the Harmonic-sieve pitch extraction method.

Contributor: Andrej Ljolje.

References

[Dubnowski, Schafer and Rabiner 76]
Dubnowski, J.J., Schafer, R.W., Rabiner, L.R.
Real-Time Digital Hardware Pitch Detector.
IEEE Trans. ASSP 24(1):2, 1976.

[Duifhuis et al. 82]
Duifhuis, H., Willems, L.F. and Sluyter, R.J.
Measurement of pitch in speech: an implementation of Goldstein's
theory of pitch perception.
JASA 71(6):1568, 1982.

[Gold 64]
Gold, B.
Note on Buzz–Hiss Detection.
JASA 36(9):1659, 1964.

[Gold and Rabiner 69]
Gold, B. and Rabiner, L.
Parallel Processing Techniques for estimating Pitch Periods of Speech
in the Time Domain.
JASA 46(2):442, 1969.

179. PLAN RECOGNITION

Alias: **plan inference**.

Given a sequence of actions carried out in a task domain by some actor, and given the actor's main goal, then the actor's plan can be inferred by a technique of working both top-down and bottom-up. A top-down elaborated **plan** is matched to the action trace and revised as appropriate. The revisions required are similar to those needed to overcome interdependent **subgoals <243>** or errors in **plan execution**. This idea has been applied in a natural language context to recognise the intention of an agent.

Contributor: Jim Doran.

References

[Allen and Perrault 80]
Allen, J. and Perrault, C.
Analyzing Intention in Utterances.
Artificial Intelligence 15:143–178, 1980.

[Schmidt, Sridharan and Goodson 78]
Schmidt, C.F., Sridharan, N.S. and Goodson, J.L.
The Plan Recognition Problem.
Artificial Intelligence 11, 1978.

180. PLAN STRUCTURE

A plan structure embodies a partially or totally ordered set of partially instantiated **operators <164>** together with the (sub) goals to which they are directed, and information which indicates how the planning environment is predicted to change as the plan is executed.

Contributor: Jim Doran.

Reference

[Nilsson 80]   Nilsson, N. J.
                 Principles of Artificial Intelligence.
                 Tioga Pub. Co., 1980.

181. POP-2

POP-2 is a programming language designed by RM Burstall and RJ Popplestone at Edinburgh University during the late 1960's. As a language intended for use in artificial intelligence research, POP-2 is conversational and provides extensive facilities for non-numerical as well as numerical applications.

The features of POP-2 include:

- a full but simple syntax, allowing immediate execution and incremental compilation, with dynamic scoping of identifiers;

- a program module facility;

- data class definition with full run time type checking. These classes can be defined by program. A wide range of standard data structures, such as lists and arrays, is provided;

- automatic garbage collection;

- primitives are provided for back-tracking, coroutining and non-local jumps;

- functions are objects that can be manipulated by the program. They can be created by program, assigned as values to variables, and passed as arguments to and returned as results from other functions (or themselves). The "closure" facility is particularly useful for function creation. As the internal structure of a function body is not accessible to the user, a significant amount of compilation can be done, providing good run-time speed without loss of flexibility. There are no separate interpreter and compiler modes.

Since the language was initially defined it has evolved considerably, and there are now two distinct dialects: WPOP on the DECsystem-10 and POP-11 on the VAX.

WPOP is supported at Edinburgh University.

    Contributor: Robert Rae.

Availability

Environment: DEC-10/TOPS-10 (64K), PDP-11/Unix version 6/7 (64Kb)

From: The Software Secretary,
      Department of Artificial Intelligence,
      University of Edinburgh,
      Forrest Hill,
      Edinburgh EH1 2QL,
      Scotland.

      Tel: 031-667-1011 x2555

Reference

[Burstall, Collins and Popplestone 71]
                Burstall, R.M., Collins J.S. and Popplestone, R.J.
                Programming in POP-2.
                Edinburgh University Press, 1971.

182. POP-11

A language developed at Sussex University for AI research and teaching, based largely on **POP-2**, but with a variety of extensions including considerably enriched syntax, built-in **pattern matching <174>**, autoloadable library files, enhanced versions of sections, processes, accessible compiler subroutines, control facilities, etc. (There is a more primitive PDP-11 Unix version which does not have all these features.) POP-11, unlike most AI languages, has been designed to be suitable for both absolute beginners, including humanities students, and advanced researchers. It comes with a large collection of teaching programs and documentation files. See **POPLOG <183>** for further details.

    Contributor: Aaron Sloman.

183. POPLOG

An interactive machine independent, multi-language, programming environment, with integral screen editor, help facility, teaching facility, etc. developed at Sussex University for teaching and research. There are three languages at present, **POP-11 <182>**, **Prolog <196>** and **LISP <34>**, all with incremental compilers. This facilitates the design of programs which use Prolog for high level problem-solving and LISP or POP-11 for deterministic lowlevel processing. On the VAX version, programs written in other languages (e.g. for efficiency) can be linked in to POPLOG. Most of the system is written in POP-11 and is therefore machine independent. All languages compile to a common virtual machine language, and compiler subroutines are available, making it easy to write compilers for other languages. (E.g. incremental compilers may be provided for **PASCAL** and FORTRAN later.) The screen editor, VED is used for program development, for accessing teaching and documentation files, and for text processing. POPLOG is being used for teaching complete beginners and for advanced research and development in universities and in industry, including speech processing, image interpretation, consistency checking of axioms in 'naive physics', and building expert systems. At present it runs only on VAX computers, but implementations are planned for the PERQ and other machines.

Contributor: Aaron Sloman.

Availability

Commercially available with documentation and support.

Environment: DEC VAX (730,750,780) and Systime VAX-lookalike with
    VMS, Berkeley Unix 4.1 (4.2 forthcoming).
    M68000: Bleasdale/Unisoft Unix (UNIPLUS), SUN-2 (forthcoming).

From: Dr Aaron Sloman,
    Cognitive Studies Programme,
    University of Sussex,
    Falmer,
    Brighton BN1 9QN,
    England.

    Tel: (0273) 606755

References

A description is available from: A Sloman, Cognitive Studies Programme, Arts E, University of Sussex, Brighton BN1 9QN, England.

184. PORTABLE STANDARD LISP

Alias: **Standard Lisp**.

PSL (Portable Standard LISP) is a new LISP implemented at the University of Utah as a successor to the various Standard LISP systems we previously distributed. PSL has about the power, speed and flavor of Franz LISP or MACLISP, with growing influence from Common LISP. It is recognized as an efficient and portable LISP implementation with many more capabilities than described in the 1979 Standard LISP report.

PSL's efficiency and portability is obtained by writing essentially all of PSL in itself, and using an optimizing compilerdriven by tables describing the target hardware and softwear environment. A standard PSL distribution includes all the sources needed to build, modify and maintain PSL on that machine, together with the executables and a manual. PSL has a machine oriented "mode" for systems programming in LISP (SYSLISP) that permits access to the target machine about as efficiently as in C or PASCAL. This mode provides for significant speed up of user programs.

PSL is in heavy use at Utah, and by collaborators at Hewlett-Packard, Rand, Stanford and other sites. Many existing programs and applications have been adapted

96

to PSL including Hearn's REDUCE computer algebra system and GLISP, Novak's object oriented LISP dialect. These are available from Hearn and Novak.

Contributor: John Campbell.

Availability

Commercially available with documentation.

Environment: DEC-20, VAX/Berkeley Unix and Apollo Domain.
VAX VMS, CRAY-1, IBM 370 forthcoming.

From: Loretta Cruse,
Pass Project Secretary,
3160 M.E.B.,
Computer Science Department,
University of Utah,
Salt Lake City UT 84112,
USA.

Tel: (801) 581-5017
Electronic address: cruse@utah-20, harpo!utah-cs!cruse (UUCP)

References

[Griss and Benson 82]
Griss, M.L. and Benson, E.
PSL: a Portable LISP System.
In *Proceedings of the 1982 ACM Symposium on LISP and Functional Programming*, pages pp 88-97. ACM, 1982.

[Griss and Hearn 81]
Griss, M.L. and Hearn, A.C.
A Portable Lisp Compiler.
Softwear Practice and Experience II:541-605, June, 1981.

185. POSTULATING INTRINSIC PROPERTIES

Given two symbolic independent variables X and Y, and one numeric dependent variable Z, one cannot find a numeric law relating these terms (since only one is numeric). However, suppose that by holding X constant and varying Y, one observes different values for Z. Then one can postulate an intrinsic property I whose values are set to those of Z, and one can associate these numeric values with the symbolic values of Y. Since one now has two numeric terms Z and I, one can find the law $Z/I = 1.0$ (which is true tautologically). However, when a new value of X is examined and the same values of Y are used, one can retrieve the intrinsic values associated with Y. In this new context the ratio Z/I may take on some other constant value, which is an empirically meaningful law. This method can be used to infer intrinsic properties such as mass, specific heat, and the index of refraction from combinations of symbolic and numeric observations.

Contributor: Pat Langley.

References

[Bradshaw, Langley and Simon 80]
> Bradshaw, G., Langley, P. and Simon H.A.
> The discovery of intrinsic properties.
> In *Proc. of the Third Nat. Conf.*. Canadian Soc for Computational Studies of Intelligence, 1980.

[Langley, Bradshaw and Simon 83]
> Langley, P., Bradshaw, G. and Simon, H.,A.
> Rediscovering chemistry with the BACON system.
> In R. Michalski, J. Carbonell, and T. Mitchell (editor), *Machine Learning: An Artificial Intelligence View*, . Tioga Press, 1983.

186. PRECONDITION ANALYSIS

Precondition Analysis is an analytic strategy-learning technique. Preconditions Analysis operates in two phases: the learning cycle and the performance cycle. In the learning cycle, the program is given an example of a correctly executed task.

The example may contain several individual steps, each step being the application of an **operator**. The program first examines the example, to find out which operators were used in performing the task. This stage is called Operator Identification. During this phase, the program may discover that it doesn't possess the relevant operator, and the user is asked to provide the necessary information.

Once this phase is complete the program builds an explanation of the strategic reasons for each step of the task. The explanation is in terms of satisfying the preconditions of following steps.

From this explanation, it builds a plan that is used by the performance element. These plans are called schemas. The performance element executes the schemas in a flexible way, using the explanation to guide it. The explanations are used to make sensible patches if the plan can't be used directly.

Precondition Analysis has been implemented in LP (Learning PRESS), a program that learns new techniques for solving algebraic equations.

Contributor: Bernard Silver.

References

[Silver 83]
> Silver, B.
> Learning Equation Solving Methods from Examples.
> In Bundy, A. (editor), *Proceedings of the Eighth IJCAI*, pages 429-431. International Joint Conference on Artificial Intelligence, 1983.

[Silver 84]
> Silver, B.
> Precondition Analysis: Learning Equation Solving Strategies from Worked Examples.
> In Michalski, R.S., Carbonell, J.G. and Mitchell, T.M. (editors), *Machine Learning 2*, . Tioga Publishing Company, 1984.

187. PREDICTIVE PARSING

Alias: **expectation-based parsing**.

Predictive parsing is an approach to natural language analysis based on the use of powerful programs associated primarily with individual lexical items which embody expectations about the form and content of the subsequent sentence/text input. The expectations are intended to determine the analysis of further inputs by providing semantic structures into which they must fit. (These structures may be those of **preference semantics <190>**, **conceptual dependency <36>**, or, by generalisation, **scripts <223>**.) The essentially word-driven basis, and emphasis on semantic rather than syntactic information and processing, of this style of parsing makes it predictive in a very different sense from that of classical top-down syntactic parsing; and allowing the exploitation of any type or piece of information in a word program offers great flexibility. The price includes a lack of generality, and overlaps or gaps between individual programs. The approach is therefore best suited to domain-limited language processing.

The main application of expectation-based parsing has been in the extraction of conceptual dependency structures from English; the technique has also been generalised in the direct application of scripts to parsing. Word expert **parsing** is a specialisation of this approach confined to word-based expectations, but not restricted to left-to-right operation.

Contributor: Karen Sparck Jones.

Reference

[Birnbaum and Selfridge 81]
Birnbaum, L., Selfridge M.
Conceptual Analysis of Natural Language.
In Schank, R.C. and Riesbeck C.K. (editor), *Inside Computer Understanding*, . LawrenceErlbaumAssociates, 1981.

188. PROCEDURAL ATTACHMENT

Alias: **procedural embedding**.

It is often necessary in knowledge representation for an executable procedure to be directly associated with one or more data structures in order to indicate when it should be used. Attached procedures lie dormant until certain conditions are satisfied, at which point they are executed. In **KRL <115>** two types of attached procedures were identified (but these hold for most systems):

(i) **servants**: these are executed when a procedure is required to apply some operation to a data object (or set of data objects), a selection mechanism may be required to select the correct procedure if more than one servant is available;

(ii) **demons <51>**: these are invoked when something has been done or is about to be done. (note that all demons whose conditions are met are activated).

Two methods of attachment were identified:

(i) **traps**: these are procedures attached to individual data objects and apply to operations and events involving the unit to which they are attached;

(ii) **triggers**: these are procedures attached to classes of data objects and apply to operations and events involving any objects in the class to which they are attached.

Both traps and triggers may be either servants or demons. (c.f "methods" in **CONNIVER** <38> and "theorems" in **Micro-PLANNER** <143>.)

Contributor: Robert Corlett.

Reference

[Bobrow and Winograd 77]
> Bobrow, D.G. and Winograd, T.
> An Overview of KRL, a Knowledge Representation Language.
> *Cognitive Science* 1:3-46, 1977.

189. PREDICATE CALCULUS

Alias: **predicate logic, first-order logic.**

Predicate calculus is a formal language in which it is possible to express statements about simple domains. It comprises a set of symbols, and rules for combining these into terms and formulae. There are also rules of **inference**, which state how a new formula can be derived from old formulae. A logical system will have an initial set of sentences ("axioms") and any sentence which can be derived from these axioms using the inference rules is called a "theorem" of the system.

The standard logic is a well-defined notation in which exact descriptive statements can be formulated about any "model" (i.e. set of objects with relations between them). Moreover, purely formal manipulations of these symbolic statements (i.e. inference) can be used to produce further valid descriptions of that same model, without direct reference to the model itself.

Terms can be constants (names of objects), variables (marking which part of a formula is quantified) or functions applied to arguments (e.g. $f(a,b,x)$). Atomic sentences are formed by applying a predicate to a set argument term (e.g. $P(f(a,b,x),c,g(h(y)))$). Compound sentences can be formed by adding negation to a sentence (e.g. ~$R(a,b)$), joining two statements with a **connective** such as $\land$ ("and"), $\lor$ ("or"), $\rightarrow$ ("implication").

There are two **quantifiers** which, used together with variables, allow the expression of universal statements:

$(\forall x) Q(x)$: "for all x, $Q(x)$"

and existential statements:

$(\exists z) R(z, a)$: "there exists a z such that $R(z, a)$"

Automatic inference techniques (e.g. **resolution** <212>) for first-order logic have been widely explored.

Contributor: Graeme Ritchie.

References

[Chang and Keisler 37]
> Chang, C.C. and Keisler, A.J.
> *Model Theory.*
> North-Holland, 1937.

[Crossley et al. 72]
> Crossley et al.
> *What is Mathematical Logic?*
> Oxford University Press, 1972.

190. PREFERENCE SEMANTICS

Approach to language understanding most fully developed by Wilks, though the basic idea is found elsewhere. The principle is that, in general, semantic constraints on word combinations cannot be absolute, as this would be incompatible with the creativity of language. The semantic patterns embodied e.g. in **case frames** <28>, and expressed e.g. by **semantic primitives** <228> indicate the mutual contextual preferences of words: for example "hit" meaning STRIKE prefers a HUMAN Agent. Word sense and sentence structure selection in text processing is then determined by maximum preference satisfaction, and does not depend on complete satisfaction.

Contributor: Karen Sparck Jones.

Reference

[Wilks 75]
> Wilks, Y.A.
> A preferential, pattern seeking semantics for natural language inference.
> *Artificial Intelligence* 6: 53-74, 1975.

191. PRIMAL SKETCH

A term used by Marr for a representation making explicit the properties of intensity changes in the retinal image(s). The Raw Primal Sketch makes explicit only very localised properties, such as size, position and orientation; the Full Primal Sketch, resulting from grouping elements of the Raw Primal Sketch, makes explicit more global properties such as alignment. Marr claimed that higher level processes interact only with the primal sketch and its derivatives, not with the data from which the primal sketch is derived. The primal sketch is computed by dedicated processors which are independent of higher level processes.

Contributors: T P Pridmore, S R Pollard, S P Stenton.

Reference

[Marr 82]   Marr, D.
              Vision.
              Freeman, 1982.

192. PRODUCTION RULE SYSTEM

Alias: Production System.

A programming language in which the programs consist of condition => action rules. The programs are interpreted by a repetition of the following operations: all rules whose conditions are satisfied are found, one of them is selected, and its action is called. Such systems have been extensively used in computational psychology and knowledge engineering.

Contributor: Alan Bundy.

Reference

[Newell and Simon 72]
              Newell, A. and Simon, H.A.
              Human Problem Solving.
              Prentice Hall, 1972.

193. PROGRAM SYNTHESIS

The derivation of a program to meet a given specification. The specification expresses conditions that the program must satisfy, but does not need to give an algorithm or method. The program is typically derived in such a way that its correctness with respect to the specification is guaranteed.

Contributor: Richard Waldinger.

194. PROGRAM TRANSFORMATION

A technique for developing programs. An initial specification is written as a probably inefficient, program and then transformed to an efficient version using methods guaranteed to preserve the meaning of the program. Within the **declarative languages** program transformations can be based on a small set of probably correct basic transformations facilitating the development of semi-automatic transformation systems.

Contributor: John Darlington.

195. PROGRAMMING CLICHE

Alias: Idiom.

Inspection methods are problem solving techniques which rely upon recognising the form of a solution. In programming there is a set of standard forms from which a wide range of programs can be constructed. This set of standard forms includes such things as particular control strategies with unspecified primitive actions. Such standard forms are know as programming cliches. The term originates from the MIT Programmer's Apprentice project. As a result of being more abstract, programming cliches are much more adaptable concepts than macros or subroutines.

Contributor: Kevin Poulter.

References

[Perlis and Rugaber 79]
          Perlis, A.J, and Rugaber, S.
          Programming with Idioms in APL.
          In *APL79 Conf. Proc.*, *Rochester N.Y.*.   , 1979.

[Rich and Waters 81]
          Rich, C. and Waters, R.C.
          Abstraction, Inspection and Debugging in Programming.
          AI Memo 634, MIT AI Lab., June, 1981.

196. PROLOG

A simple but powerful and practical programming language based on the idea of programming in logic. PROLOG programs may be viewed as logical clauses and the interpreter as an efficient resolution theorem prover. PROLOG may be looked on as an extension of LISP <34> in that it provides as primitives **pattern directed procedure** invocation <173> and **non-determinism** (backtracking). It provides general recursive (tree-like) data structures which are accessed by pattern-matching rather than by explicit selector functions. There are no destructive operations on these data structures, but structures may contain empty slots (uninstantiated logical variables) which can be filled in later. There is also an **assertional database** which is used for relatively long-lived or permanent data.

PROLOG implementations exist on a large number of different computers. Currently the most efficient of these is due to David Warren and runs on the DEC-10 [Bowen et al 82]. It includes a compiler, rather than just an interpreter, and has been shown to be comparable in efficiency with compiler-based LISP systems [Warren, Pereira and Pereira]. For an introductory textbook for PROLOG see [Clocksin and Mellish 81].

Contributor: David Bowen.

Availability

Commercially available with documentation and support.

Environment: DEC-10/20

From: The Software Secretary,
      Department of Artificial Intelligence,
      University of Edinburgh,
      Forrest Hill,
      Edinburgh EH1 2QL,
      Scotland.

      Tel: 031-667-1011 x2555

References

[Bowen, et al. 82]
            Bowen et al.
            Decsystem-10 PROLOG User's Manual
            Dept. of Artificial Intelligence, Edinburgh, 1982.
            Occasional Paper 27.

[Clocksin and Mellish 81]
            Clocksin, W.F. and Mellish, C.S.
            Programming in Prolog.
            Springer Verlag, 1981.

[Warren, Pereira and Pereira 77]
            Warren, D.H.D., Pereira, L.M., and Pereira, F.
            Prolog – the language and its implementation compared with Lisp.
            In *ACM Symposium on AI and Programming Languages.*   Association
                for Computing Machinery, 1977.

197. PROPAGATION IN CELLULAR ARRAYS

One particular facet of the use of parallel cellular arrays for image processing is that the physical interconnection structure of the array can reflect the supposed connectivity of images.   This approach is most useful when the array allows "global propagation".   That is propagation of signals from pixel groups across arbitrary distances, with each intermediate **pixel** transforming the signal according to its local data.   For example global propagation allows a **CLIP** series machine to extract a labelled component of a binary image of arbitrary complexity in one machine cycle. See also **relaxation labelling <210>** and **cellular arrays <29>**.

Contributor: Dave Reynolds.

Reference

[Otto 82]   Otto G.P.
                Counting and Labelling Objects on CLIP4.
                Report 82/11, Image Processing Group, Dept. of Physics and
                    Astronomy, University College London, 1982.

104

198. PROPERTY LISTS

A technique whereby a list of name-value pairs is associated with an object (such as a node of a **semantic net <227>**). Each name represents a certain attribute of the object and the corresponding value records the value of that attribute assigned to the object. Such a facility for associating property lists with atoms is provided as a primitive operation in **LISP <34>** type languages.

Contributor: Lincoln Wallen.

Reference

[Allen 78]   Allen, J.
               Anatomy of LISP.
               McGraw-Hill, 1978.

199. PROPOSITIONAL CONSTRAINT PROPAGATION

A propositional constraint is a **resolution** clause all of whose atoms are simple sentential variables. Propositional constraint propagation is an incomplete inference procedure which operates on propositional constraints and is equivalent to unit clause **resolution <212>**.

Contributor: D. McAllester.

Reference

[McAllester 80] McAllester, D.
                 An Outlook on Truth Maintenance.
                 AI Memo 551, MIT AI Lab., August, 1980.

200. PROTOCOL ANALYSIS

A technique for extracting the procedures used by a human problem solver from a record of selected aspects of his/her problem solving behaviour. The record may be of verbal behaviour (e.g. a "think-aloud protocol") or of non-verbal behaviour (e.g. eye-movements, or the sequence and timing of moves in a board game). The analysis begins with the building of a **Problem Behaviour Graph** which serves as a "rational reconstruction" of the solution steps. Regularities are then sought and extracted, possibly in the form of a **production rule system <192>**. Protocol analysis remains an art learned by apprenticeship.

Contributor: Richard Young.

References

[Ericsson and Simon 80]
                Ericsson, K.A. and Simon, H.A.
                Verbal reports as data.
                Psychological Review 87:215-251, 1980.

[Newell 77]   Newell, A.
On the analysis of human problem solving protocols.
In Johnson-Laird, P.N. & Wason, P.C. (editor), *Thinking: Readings in Cognitive Science*, . Cambridge U.P., 1977.
excerpt.

201. PSI

PSI is a knowledge based **program synthesis <193>** system developed at Stanford. The synthesis module consists of two major sub-systems:

1. **PECOS**, the coding expert, is a set of refinement rules for program synthesis which represent a range of knowledge about sets, xmappings, arrays, etc.

2. **LIBRA**, the efficiency expert, consists of knowledge which enables the system to evaluate alternative implementations of a program.

The complete PSI system has synthesised the code for a simple version of a learning program.

Contributor: Kevin Poulter.

<u>References</u>

[Barstow 79]   Barstow, D.
Knowledge-Based Program Construction.
Elsevier North Holland, New York, 1979.
The Computer Science Library, Programming Language Series.

[Kant 81]   Kant, E.
Efficiency in Program Synthesis.
Technical Report Computer Science: Artificial Intelligence, No. 8, UMI Research Press, Ann Arbor, Michigan, 1981.

202. PYRAMIDS/RESOLUTION CONES

Strictly, a pyramid/resolution cone is a set of arrays used to store a digitised image at different resolutions, the highest resolution forming the base of the pyramid. Normally, there is a uniform relationship between adjacent levels of the pyramid, for example, a pixel intensity at a particular resolution is often the average value of the pixel intensities in the corresponding 2 x 2 pixel block at the next highest resolution. More generally, the concept of a regular hierarchical data structure has been extended to include processing elements within the structure, then known as a **processing cone**. Originally, pyramids were used to explicate the relationship between the different image resolutions in a computer vision system using planning. For instance, the boundaries found at a low resolution might be used to refine the **edge detection<65>/ boundary detection <21>** process at higher resolutions. This can significantly improve the efficiency of the overall edge detection process. More recently, it has been realised that image boundaries occur over a wide range of scales from sharp step-like edges to fuzzy, blurred edges. Some results have been stated on using the relationships between corresponding edges occurring at different resolutions to make assertions about the scene boundary producing them. Since these regular hierarchical structures are inappropriate for non-spatial symbolic computation their use is normally restricted to the early processing stage of a vision system.

Contributor: Bob Beattie.

Reference

[Tanimoto 78]   Tanimoto, S.L.
                 Regular Hierarchical Image and Processing Structures in Machine
                     Vision.
                 In Hanson, A.H. and Riseman, E.M. (editor), *Computer Vision
                     Systems*, . Academic Press Inc., 1978.

203. QLISP/QA4

QA4 developed from a series of languages based on the semantics of theorem provers.   It was an attempt to provide a language whereby the programmer could encode **domain specific knowledge** in such a way as to guide the underlying theorem prover to a proof.   A version of QA4 was implemented in **INTERLISP** <103>, called QLISP.

QLISP combines all the data structures of INTERLISP with the special data structures af QA4.   These are classes, **bags**, **vectors**, and tuples.   Classes are sets (i.e. unordered collections of distinct elements) and bags are like sets except that multiple occurrences of elements are allowed.   A vector in QLISP is a list of fixed length and tuples are vectors where the first element is a function.   In order to do efficient **pattern matching** <174> for data retrieval every item in the database is stored in canonical form in a **discrimination net** <59>.   Since every subexpression of an expression is also stored separately in the net, QLISP suffers from an excessive use of space.   The pattern matching is based on an algorithm for **unification** <252> and unlike **PLANNER** <143> and **CONNIVER** <38> allows the variables in both the target and the pattern to be instantiated during matching.   (c.f.   **PROLOG** <196> and **theorem proving** programs.)

Properties can be associated with **assertions** (facts) and theorems (which come in the same flavours as the PLANNER and CONNIVER theorems: **if-added**, **if-removed** and **if-needed**).   Indeed the truth of an assertion or theorem is not denoted merely by its presence in the database but by its model value which can take the values T or NIL (for true or false).   The invocation of a procedure (theorem) may then be based on these properties.   Each goal statement can contain an apply team denoting the class of consequent theorems that should be invoked to try to solve the goal.   The attention of the theorem prover may be drawn to relevant facts and theorems in this way.   QLISP supports **context** mechanisms like those of **CONNIVER**.

Contributor: Lincoln Wallen.

Reference

[Rulifson, Waldinger and Derkson 71]
Rulifson, J. F., Waldinger, R. A., and Derkson, J.A.
A language for writing problem-solving programs.
In *Proceedings of IFIPS Congress '71, Ljubljana, Yugoslavia*. IFIPS,
1971.

204. QUAD TREES

A hierarchical image representation similar to **pyramids <202>**, they have nodes that correspond to the cells of a pyramid and each non-terminal node has four children, but unlike a pyramid, a quad tree may be pruned so as to be unbalanced. For example, when all nodes in a subtree have the same gray value, the subtree may be represented by its root without loss of information, so that significant storage savings can be obtained for many images. More significantly, quad trees allow some operations to be performed efficiently by recursive procedures.

Contributor: Luis Jenkins.

Reference

(Cohen and Feigenbaum 82)
Cohen, P. and Feigenbaum, E. (editors).
The Handbook of Artificial Intelligence Vol. 3.
Kaufmann, 1982.

205. RAPT

RAPT is an object level language for programming assembly robots offline. The emphasis is on describing spatial relationships that should be made to hold between surface features of the objects being assembled ("bottom of plate against top of block") and on describing movements of objects relative to their features ("move bolt parallel to shaft of bolt"). A powerful inference system is needed to convert descriptions at this level into descriptions in terms of the actual positions the objects (including the manipulators) must take up in order to achieve these relationships. RAPT has been implemented with two different inference systems — one using algebraic manipulation of position expressions and the other using reduction of relational networks using **rewrite rules <213>**.

Contributor: Pat Ambler.

Availability

Environment:

From: The Software Secretary,
      Department of Artificial Intelligence,
      University of Edinburgh,
      Forrest Hill,
      Edinburgh EH1 2QL,
      Scotland.

Tel: 031-667-1011 x2555

References

[Popplestone and Ambler 80]
        Popplestone, R.J. and Ambler, A.P.
        An efficient and portable implementation of RAPT.
        In *1st ICAA Brighton*.   Int Fluidics Services, 1980.

[Popplestone, Ambler and Bellos 80]
        Popplestone, R.J., Ambler, A.P. and Bellos, I.M.
        An interpreter for a language for describing assemblies.
        Artificial Intelligence 14, 1980.

206. REFLECTANCE MAP

A reflectance map relates image intensities to surface orientation for given reflectance function, viewpoint and illumination direction.   It is usually possible to construct a reflectance map for a surface even under complicated illumination conditions though it may be necessary to measure the intensities empirically as the relation is frequently too complex to be modelled analytically.   See also **intrinsic images <105>**.

Contributors: T P Pridmore, S R Pollard, S P Stenton.

Reference

[Horn 77]   Horn, B.K.P.
               Understanding Image Intensities.
               Artificial Intelligence 8: 201-231, 1977.

207. REFUTATION PROOF

Alias: **proof by contradiction, reductio ad absurdum**.

A method of **proof** in which the conjecture is negated and a contradiction deduced thus proving the conjecture to be true.   This is the method of proof utilised by most **resolution <212>** theorem provers.

Contributor: Dave Plummer.

Reference

[Nilsson 80]   Nilsson, N.J.
               Principles of Artificial Intelligence.
               Tioga Pub. Co., 1980.

208. REGION FINDING

Alias: **region growing**.

The basic idea of region finding is to produce a **segmentation** of the image in which the regions (connected sets of pixels) found have a useful correspondence to projections of scene entities such as objects or surfaces. As such it is the (currently unpopular) dual of **edge detection <65>/boundary detection <21>**. There are two main approaches:

- Start with the maximum number of regions (eg make every pixel a region) and merge adjacent regions based on some measure of similarity until a satisfactory **segmentation** has been achieved.

- Start with a few (possibly one) large regions and recursively split them into smaller regions based on some measure of dissimilarity until a satisfactory segmentation has been achieved.

Measures of similarity/dissimilarity have ranged from simple average intensities to complex methods incorporating semantics.

Contributor: Bob Beattie.

References

[Ballard and Brown 82]
> Ballard, D. H. and Brown, C. M.
> *Computer Vision.*
> Prentice-Hall International Inc., 1982.

[Zucker 76]   Zucker, S.W.
> Region Growing: Childhood and Adolescence.
> *Computer Graphics and Image Processing* 5:382-399, 1976.

209. RELATIONAL DATABASE QUERY FORMULATION

A technique for specifying queries and other interactions against the Relational and Entity-Relationship Data Models. Database semantics are initially presented as a hierarchy of Functional Areas, leading to Entity- Relationship/Relational description. A naive-user mode provides system initiated dialogue with natural language statements of queries (i.e. paraphrases of Relational Calculus expressions) displayed for user validation. Self-teaching system, with simple `user controlled' inferencing.

Contributor: Jim Longstaff.

Reference

[Longstaff 82]   Longstaff, J.
Controlled Inference and Instruction Techniques for DBMS Query
Languages.
In *P111 Proceedings of 1982 ACM SIGMOD Conference*.   Association
for Computing Machinery, 1982.

210. RELAXATION LABELLING

Relaxation labelling is a technique for assigning globally consistent labels or
values to nodes in a network subject to local constraints, by iteratively propagating
the effects of **constraints <39>** through the net.   It has its mathematical origins as a
technique in numerical analysis for the solution of difference equations and recent
developments have shown it to be related to various optimisation techniques eg.
linear programming.   The first significant application of relaxation labelling to a
vision problem was Waltz's **filtering algorithm** in the blocks world **line labelling**
domain.   Consider the problem of assigning labels to objects to satisfy certain
consistency requirements.   Unlike a tree representation where each context is
explicitly a path, the space may be represented as a graph in which each node
carries a set of possible labels.   The task is to find a single labelling for each
node that satisfies the set of constraints.   In general, after an initialisation stage in
which each node has been assigned a list of labels and their associated
confidence measures, the labels and confidences of neighbouring nodes are
compared and, guided by the requirement to minimise local inconsistency (often a
smoothness constraint), labels are deleted or their confidences adjusted.   This
process of comparison and adjustment iterates until it converges to some criterion of
global consistency.   Because both the assignment and updating processes can be
done independently at each node, the computation is inherently parallel.

Apart from Waltz's classical application, relaxation labelling has been used in the
computation of **optical flow**, the recovery of surface orientation from
shading information, and the recovery of the orientation structure of images,
stereopsis and structure from **motion**.   The convergence properties of some relaxation
operators are not always transparent.   The most successful and scientifically useful
applications have been when the theoretical analysis of a vision problem reveals a
mathematical structure that can be directly exploited in the design of the relaxation
algorithm rather than when a "general operator" has been fitted in an ad hoc
fashion to a vision labelling task.   See also propagation in **cellular arrays <29>**.

Contributor: Jon Mayhew.

References

[Ballard and Brown 82]
Ballard, D. H. and Brown, C. M.
Computer Vision.
Prentice-Hall International Inc., 1982.

[Davis and Rosenfeld 81]
Davis, L.S. and Rosenfeld, A.
Cooperating processes in low level.
Artificial Intelligence 17:246-265, 1981.

211. REMOTE PROCEDURE CALLS

A remote procedure call is a conceptually simple way of tying together a multi-machine system. As its name suggests, it is like an ordinary procedure call, but the called procedure need not reside in the same machine as the calling code. The idea is that the semantics of a remote procedure should be the same as the semantics of a local procedure call, thus considerably simplifying the task of constructing multi-machine systems, both conceptually and practically.

Contributor: Henry Thompson.

Reference

[Bruce 81]   Bruce, N.
Remote Procedure Call.
Technical Report CSL-81-9, Xerox Palo Alto Research Center, 1981.

212. RESOLUTION

A **rule of inference** of **predicate calculus <189>** used to deduce a new formula from two old ones. It has been used extensively in **automatic theorem proving**, because it is an efficient alternative to traditional rules of inference in mathematical logic. All the three formulae involved must be in **clausal form <33>**. If C and D are **clauses** and the P_i and Q_j are atomic formulae then the rule is

$$\frac{C \lor P_1 \lor \ldots \lor P_m}{(C \lor D)\sigma}$$
$$D \lor \neg Q_1 \lor \ldots \lor \neg Q_m$$

where σ is the most general **unifier** of all the P_i and Q_j, and is obtained by **unification <252>**.

Contributor: Alan Bundy.

Reference

[Chang and Lee 73]
Chang, C. and Lee, R.C.
Symbolic Logic and Mechanical Theorem Proving.
Academic Press, 1973.

213. REWRITE RULES

Alias: **condition-action pairs, demodulants.**

Rewrite rules are sets of ordered pairs of expressions (lhs,rhs) usually depicted as (lhs => rhs). There is usually a similarity relation between the "lhs" and the "rhs" such as equality, inequality or double implication. Rewrite rules, as the pairs are called, together with the rewriting **rule of inference** allow one expression to be "rewritten" into another. A subexpression of the initial expression is matched with the "lhs" of the rewrite rule yielding a **substitution**. The resulting expression is the expression obtained by replacing the distinguished subexpression with the "rhs" of the rewrite rule after applying the substitution.

The matching process may be full **unification <252>** or, more usually, a restricted form of **pattern matching <174>** where only the variables in the rewrite rule may be instantiated. Examples of the use of rewrite rules are the restricted paramodulation **<170>** inferences called demodulation performed in theorem provers or programming with abstract data types introduced by a series of equations. Some powerful theoretical results have been obtained for rewriting systems.

Contributor: Lincoln Wallen.

Reference

[Huet & Oppen 80]
> Huet, G. and Oppen, D. C.
> *Equations and Rewrite Rules: A Survey.*
> Technical Report CSL-111, SRI International, January, 1980.

214. RLL

A structured collection of tools to help the **knowledge engineer** construct, use and modify expert systems, written in **INTERLISP <103>**. RLL is in itself an **expert system**, knowledgeable in facts about programming in general, and its own routines in particular. RLL contains a collection of useful constructs, including different types of **slots**, control mechanisms and inheritance **schemes**. Control is via an **agenda** mechanism.

Contributor: Luis Jenkins.

References

[Greiner and Lenat 80]
> Greiner, R. and Lenat, D.B.
> A Representation Language Language.
> In *Proc. First Annual National Conference on Artificial Intelligence,*
> pages 165-169. American Association for Artificial Intelligence,
> 1980.

[Waterman and Hayes-Roth 82]
> Waterman, D. and Hayes-Roth, F.
> *An Investigation of Tools for Building Expert Systems.*
> Technical Report R-2818-NSF, Rand Corporation, June, 1982.

215. ROBMOD

An experimental **geometric modelling system** for studying **locality algorithms** under a **constructive solid geometry** framework, and in particular for studying **clash detection** with robotics in mind. Written in C it uses algorithms similar to those employed in **VOLE <259>** for picture output.

Contributor: Stephen Cameron.

Availability

Available as a research tool.

Environment: C on VAX 11/750 and ICL Perq both under Unix.

From: Steve Cameron,
      Dept. of Artificial Intelligence,
      Forrest Hill,
      Edinburgh.

      Tel: (031) 667-1011 ext. 2551

216. ROBOT DYNAMICS

Robot dynamics addresses the problems of calculating the acceleration of a robot from a given set of forces (forward dynamics), and calculating the forces required to produce a given acceleration (inverse dynamics). Forward dynamics is used for **simulation**, inverse dynamics for control. A robot is considered to be a system of rigid bodies, or links, connected together by joints. The laws of motion for rigid bodies are used to find the equations of motion for the robot. The two main approaches are via Newton's and Euler's equations, and via Lagrange's equation. The tricky part is to calculate the answers efficiently. This is done by expressing the equations of motion in terms of recurrence relations between the motion of one link and that of one of its neighbours in such a way that the answers may be calculated recursively.

Contributor: Roy Featherstone.

References

[Hollerbach 80] Hollerbach, J.M.
                 A recursive Lagrangian Formulation of Manipulator Dynamics and a
                   Comparative Study of Dynamics Formulation Complexity.
                 IEEE Trans. Systems, Man & Cybernetics SMC-10(11):730-736, 1980.

[Paul 81]   Paul, R.P.
                 Robot manipulators.
                 MIT Press, 1981.

[Walker and Orin 82]
                 Walker M.W. and Orin, D.E.
                 Efficient Dynamic Computer Simulation of Robotic Mechanisms.
                 Trans. ASME, ser. G, Jnl. Dyn. Sys. Measurement & Control
                   104:205-211, 1982.

217. ROBOT PROGRAMMING

The principle advantage of the industrial robot over conventional automation is programmability. The robot extends the capabilities of **NC machine tools <160>** by performing motions necessary for transferring parts and tools, forging, casting,

114

painting, assembly, welding, and so forth. More flexible machining operations can also be performed by robots, but at the cost of precision. The requirements of robot programming systems are in specifying motions, controlling devices, flow of control, world modelling, and specifying the use of sensors. Four levels of abstraction in robot programming can be identified: (1) actuator level, in which axis values (joint angles) are specified for each step of the task; (2) end-effector level, in which the position of the tool is specified in any of several coordinate systems such as **cartesian coordinates** and Euler angles; (3) object level, in which the task is described in terms of operations on objects ("insert pin in hole"); and (4) objective level, in which the user specifies the task in a declarative form, and is not required to specify the manner in which the task is performed. All industrial robots permit level 1 operations, and many robots have level 2 capabilities. Level 3 is currently represented by laboratory systems such as **RAPT <205>** and **AUTOPASS**. Level 4 is the subject of research: automatic planners and declarative languages such as **PROLOG <196>** may be expected to contribute to this area.

Contributor: W. F. Clocksin.

References

[Koutsou 81]   Koutsou, A.
A survey of model-based robot programming languages.
Working Paper 108, Dept. of Artificial Intelligence, Edinburgh, 1981.

[Lozano-Perez 82]
Lozano-Perez, T.
Robot programming.
Memo 698, MIT AI Lab, 1982.

218. ROSIE

A general-purpose **production rule**-based **<192>** programming system for expert systems applications with an English-like syntax, implemented in **INTERLISP <103>**. Knowledge is represented as n-ary relations and and rules can be organized in rule sets defined to be either procedures, generators or predicates. Supports three types of inference mechanisms: state-driven, goal-driven and change-driven. Has useful facilities for I/O, communications and explanation routines and a powerful **pattern matcher <174>**.

Contributor: Luis Jenkins.

References

[Fain 81]   Fain, J. et al.
The ROSIE Language Reference Manual
N-1647-ARPA edition, The Rand Corporation, 1981.

[Waterman and Hayes-Roth 82]
Waterman, D. and Hayes-Roth, F.
An Investigation of Tools for Building Expert Systems.
Technical Report R-2818-NSF, Rand Corporation, June, 1982.

219. RUP

RUP is a reasoning utility package with an **assertion interning** mechanism, a **truth maintenance system** <250>, facilities for supporting **invariant queues** <106>, a language for writing invariant **demons** <51> of various kinds, and a **congruence closure mechanism**. RUP maintains many internal invariants relating the TMS justifications, truth assignments to assertions, contradictions, equality assertions, and equivalence classes.

Contributor: D. McAllester.

Availability

Available as a research tool with documentation.

Environment: FranzLisp, InterLisp and ZetaLisp

From: David McAllester (ZetaLisp)
545 Technology Square,
Cambridge,
Mass. 02139,
USA.

Tel: (617) 253-8827
Electronic address: dam@mit-mc

FranzLisp version from: Harry Pople, University of Pittsburg

InterLisp version from: Mark Vilain, BBN

Reference

[McAllester 82] McAllester, D.
Reasoning Utility Package User's Manual Version One.
Memo 667, MIT AI Lab, April, 1982.

220. SAGE

Fully supported expert systems shell written in **PASCAL**. It has its own high level ('English-like') language for the input of **production rules** and a compiler ; the run-time system uses a disc-based compiled form of the rules. Principally **backward chaining** but with the ability to bring in new areas of rules. It can interface to user-written procedures and functions which are callable from the rules. 'English' output of advice is provided - not just numbers. There are comprehensive user-investigation facilities (WHY, FACTORS, HISTOGRAM etc.).

Contributor: Gareth Williams.

Availability

Commercially available with documentation and support. Special rates to academic institutions.

Environment: DEC VAX/VMS, DEC PDP/RSX, Prime/PRIMOS with Prime Pascal.

From: Dr. M.L. Barrett,
      SPl International,
      The Charter,
      Abingdon,
      Oxon OX14 3LZ,
      England.

      Tel: 0235-24112

Reference

[SAGE 83]   *The SAGE Language Specification*
               from: SPL Research centre, The Charter, Abingdon, Oxon., 1983.

221. SAIL

Unlike many AI languages SAIL is compiler (rather than interpreter) based. Developed on top of **ALGOL-60** it is also block structured. SAIL was originally designed with vision and speech understanding systems in mind, and incorporates a fast associative retrieval facility called **LEAP**.

SAIL incorporates all the ALGOL-60 data structures and supports user defined record types and items. Items are associative triples, each element of which may be either an identifier or another item. An item is indexed off each of its three positions thus making the retrieval process very efficient. **Pattern matching <174>** is used solely for **database retrieval**.

SAIL also has a well developed **multi-processing capability**, communication between processes being handled by a message queuing system. Any process may "sprout" another process, the ALGOL-60 scoping rules being inherited so that the child process shares the same database as the parent. A control primitive "join" suspends one process until another has terminated thus aiding synchronization.

Contributor: Lincoln Wallen.

References

[Feldman and Rovner 69]
               Feldman, J.A., and Rovner, P.D.
               An Algol-based associative language.
               Communication of the ACM 8:439-449, 1969.

[Feldman et al. 72]
               Feldman, J.A., Low, J.R., Swinehart, D.C. and Taylor, R.H.
               Recent developments in SAIL.
               Report AIM-176, AI Laboratory, Stanford University, 1972.

[Reiser 76]   Reiser, J.F.
               SAIL
               STAN-CS-76-574 edition, 1976.

222. SASL

An application language developed at St Andrews University during the period 1972-76. Is higher order, has all **type-checking** delayed until run-time (thus permitting the definition of functions with arbitrary polymorphism), supports non-strict functions and infinite data structures, has **pattern-matching** on lists and nested block structure using Landin's "where". Was probably the first language to systematically exploit the power of lazy evaluation. Also of interest is the implementation technique for SASL developed later at the University of Kent, which involves compilation to combinatory logic and has proved considerably more efficient than the earlier implementation based on an SECD machine. The combinators implementation of SASL runs under **Unix**. See also KRC <114>.

Contributor: D.A. Turner.

Availability

From: David Turner,
    University of Kent,
    Canterbury,
    England.

References

[Turner 76]   Turner, D.A.
                 SASL Language Manual.
                 Technical Report, St Andrews University, December, 1976.
                 Revised edition from University of Kent, August 1979.

[Turner 79]   Turner, D.A.
                 A New Implementation Technique for Applicative Languages.
                 Software - Practice and Experience , 1979.

223. SCRIPT

A structure for the large scale organisation of knowledge, which was introduced by Schank, primarily as a support for natural language understanding, and related to **conceptual dependency** <36> as the primary form of knowledge representation. Scripts define the normal character and sequence of events in e.g. a restaurant visit as a temporal incident. They can thus be used to assign an order to language data that do not give temporal information explicitly, and may also be used to indicate underlying causal relationships. The need for explicit inference to determine temporal or causal relations between data instances is therefore reduced. The event orientation of scripts distinguishes them from **frames** <77>, but they share other properties of frames, e.g. defaults and attached procedures, and forms of set organisation, and present similar problems of definition and use. Scripts have been applied to a wide variety of language processing tasks (e.g. **MOPS**), chiefly by the Yale group. In general, usage of the term is less variable than that of frame, but it is still applied with a good deal of freedom.

Contributor: Karen Sparck Jones.

Reference

[Schank and Abelson 77]

> Schank, R. and Abelson, R.
> *Scripts, Plans, Goals and Understanding.*
> Lawrence Erlbaum Associates, 1977.

224. SEMANTIC BINARY RELATIONSHIP MODEL

This is an information model suitable for a smart database, and also for knowledge representation when large amounts of data are expected. The SBRM is a **semantic net** <227> formed by providing a **Binary Relationship model** with several built-in entities and relationships with pre-defined semantics. These give the structural and abstraction mechanisms for classifying data and for the generalisation/specialisation of classes into hierarchies. The resulting class structure proves useful for implementing several aspects of **integrity checking**, **concurrency control**, inheritance rules and **inference**. Since the n-place predicates of logic are represented in the semantic network by (n+1) binary relationships (i.e. 2-place predicates), explicit rules may be represented in the SBRM. A version of the SBRM has been implemented in PASCAL/Unix, using the notion of associatively-accessed triples for the low-level storage.

Contributors: M. Azmodek and Simon Lavington.

Availability

Available as a research tool with documentation.

Environment: Pascal on Unix

From: S.H. Lavington,
        Dept. of Computer Science,
        University of Manchester,
        Manchester M13 9PL,
        England.

References

[Azmodek and Dunnion 84]

> Azmodek, M., and Dunnion, J.N.
> *A BRM machine and its interface procedures.*
> Internal Report IFS/4/84, Dept. of Computer Science, University of Manchester, 1984.

[Azmodek, Lavington and Standring ??]

> Azmodek, M., Lavington, S.H., and Standring, M.
> The Semantic Binary Relation Model of Information.
> To appear in the Proceedings of the 3rd joint BCS and ACM Symposium on Information Retrieval, July 1984.

225. SEMANTIC CHECKING

Alias: use of models.

A technique for pruning a **search space** of a logical inference mechanism, e.g. **resolution <212>** or **natural deduction <153>**.   One or more models are given of the axioms and hypotheses of a problem.   If the model is not a counterexample then the goal is also true in the model(s).   All subgoals false in any model are pruned from the search space.   This technique preserves completeness if the problem consists only of **Horn clauses <97>**.

Contributor: Alan Bundy.

Reference

[Gelernter 63]   Feigenbaum, E. and Feldman, J. (editors).
                 Realization of a Geometry theorem-proving machine.
                 McGraw-Hill, 1963.

226. SEMANTIC GRAMMAR

Semantic   grammar   is   contrasted   with   conventional   grammars,   by   relying predominantly on semantic rather than syntactic categories, e.g.

     MESSAGE → PATIENTTYPE HAVE DISEASETYPE

In   some   cases   the   semantic   categories   and   structures   are   merely   cosmetic relabellings of conventional syntactic categories and structures, but more thorough semantic grammars are widely used, though even these typically contain some mixture of syntactic elements.   Semantic grammars have been found especially effective for language processing in limited domain contexts, e.g.   processing medical   records,   interpreting   database   queries,   where   syntactic   parsing   is unnecessarily costly, but general-purpose semantic grammars have also been proposed.   There is a connection between these grammars and **semantic primitives <228>** and semantic **case frames <28>**.   However systems making heavy use of general-purpose semantics are not conventionally described as relying on semantic grammars.

Contributor: Karen Sparck Jones.

Reference

[Brown and Burton 75]
                 Brown, J.S. and Burton, R.
                 Multiple representations of knowledge for tutorial reasoning.
                 In Bobrow, D.G. and Collins, A. (editor), *Representation and
                 Understanding.*   Academic Press, 1975.

227. SEMANTIC NET

Alias: semantic network.

Principle for the large scale organisation of knowledge emphasising the multiple associations of individual concepts. Concepts, objects, entities, etc. are represented as **nodes** in a **linked** graph, and relationships between these are represented as labeled arcs. The range of possible network structure types is very wide (see Findler). Semantic nets should properly be based on definitions of the net structure, i.e. the syntax and semantics of nodes and links and of configurations of these, and of net operations, i.e. the syntax and semantics of node-node transitions, but too frequently are not. Nets have been found an attractive descriptive device, but genuine algorithmic exploitation of nets based e.g. on the general idea of **marker passing** for selective reading or writing at nodes, is comparatively rare. (Formal graph theory is rarely seriously invoked in artificial intelligence.) The emphasis on concept association introduces difficulties in representing any partitioning or grouping of net elements, for example to represent quantified propositions, clusters of similar entities, etc. (but see **partitioned net <172>**, and network searching conspicuously manifests the general AI problem of the **combinatorial explosion**.

Contributor: Karen Sparck Jones.

Reference

[Findler 79]   Findler, N.V. (editor).
                 Associative Networks.
                 Academic Press, 1979.

228. SEMANTIC PRIMITIVES

General concepts underlying words, used for the determination and representation of textual or propositional meaning, e.g. MOVE underlies "walk" and "run", THING "vase" and "book". Semantic primitives are used to define selection criteria for sense identification, and to define key properties e.g. of **case frame <28>** role fillers. Primitives, which should in principle be drawn from a closed set, may be shallow or deep, domain-independent or domain-dependent, categorial or relational, etc. The characterisations of word (senses) may be by single primitives, primitive sets, or structured formulae, and the primitive characterisations of sentences may be more or less elaborately structured. The primitive names may be regarded as elements of a distinct meaning representation language, or as selected elements of the language under description. Though primitives universally figure in some form or other in language understanding systems, they are more frequently adopted ad hoc than systematically motivated. Wilks and Schank are exceptions here.

Contributor: Karen Sparck Jones.

Reference

[Charniak and Wilks 76]
                 Charniak, E. and Wilks, Y.
                 Computational Semantics.
                 North-Holland, 1976.

229. SENSORY FEEDBACK AND COMPLIANCE

A common problem in robotics is to bring a tool to a certain spatial relationship to a workpiece, or to bring two or more components together into a certain spatial relationship. However, owing to accumulation of dimensional variation and tolerances that cannot be minimised at their source, errors can occur, making it unexpectedly difficult or impossible to solve this problem by dead reckoning. Thus, in many cases, a robot must be able to detect that components are poorly positioned, and it must have the ability to make small incremental changes in position to minimise the error. 'Sensing', or the measurement of physical properties (optical, acoustic, tactile, etc) can be used actively to detect displacements from the correct position; the resulting error signal is fed back to steer the robot in the direction to minimise the error. This is known as closed-loop control, which is formalised by Control Theory. Compliance is a passive control technique, where springs and other mechanical devices are used to produce corrective displacements in reaction to forces in the tool.

Contributor: W. F. Clocksin.

References

[Dorf 80]   Dorf, R. C.
               Modern Control Systems.
               Addison-Wesley, 1980.

[Nevins J. L. and Whitney D. E. 78]
               Nevins and Whitney.
               Computer controlled assembly.
               Scientific American , February, 1978.

[Simons 80]   Simons G. L.
               Robots in Industry.
               NCC Publications, 1980.

230. SHAPE ANALYSIS

A branch of binary image processing which tries to encode/describe the shape of the binary objects in an image. One approach is to decompose the object into primary convex sets. Alternatively shapes are described by a series of shape measures which progressively define the shape more and more accurately. Examples are moments of higher and higher order, and the fourier transform of the object boundary arc coordinates.

Contributor: Dave Reynolds.

Reference

[Pavlidis 77] Pavlidis T.
               Structural Pattern Recognition.
               Springer-Verlag, Berlin, 1977.

231. SHAPE FROM SHADING

The process of extracting three-dimensional shape information from smooth gradations of reflected light intensity. It has been shown by Horn that if certain assumptions are made concerning the reflectance function and illumination of a surface it is possible to formulate and solve equations relating surface shape to the measured intensities in an image of the surface. See **intrinsic images <105>**.

Contributors: T P Pridmore, S R Pollard, S T Stenton.

Reference

[Horn]   Horn, R.K.P.
               Obtaining Shape from Shading Information.
               In Winston, P.H. (editor), *The Psychology of Computer Vision*.

232. SHAPE FROM TEXTURE

Shape from texture is the process by which the three-dimensional structure of a surface is determined from the spatial distribution of surface markings. Projection into the image plane distorts the geometry of surface textures in a manner dependent upon the shape of the underlying surface: as a surface recedes from the viewer its markings appear smaller due to perspective effects, and as a surface is inclined away from the frontal plane its markings appear compressed in the direction of the inclination. By isolating these projective distortions it is possible to recover the shape of a textured surface.

Contributors: T. P. Pridmore, S. R. Pollard, S. T. Stenton.

Reference

[Witkin 81]   Witkin, A.P.
               Recovering Surface Shape and Orientation from Texture.
               Artificial Intelligence 17:17-45, 1981.

233. SITUATION CALCULUS

A technique for representing time or different situations in an assertional database. Each relation/property which changes over time is given an extra argument place, which is filled with a situation term. In **plan formation** this situation argument is usually a nested term representing the sequence of plan steps needed to get to this situation from the initial state. Thus situations label the effect of actions and can represent alternative futures, whereas a numerically measured time can only represent a unique future.

Contributor: Alan Bundy.

Reference

[Nilsson 80]   Nilsson, N.J.
                Principles of Artificial Intelligence.
                Tioga Pub. Co., 1980.

234. SKELETONISATION

This is a transformation of a binary image which locates the central axis ("skeleton" or "medial-axis") of each object in the image. The general principle is to thin each object in the image to a line structure by repeatedly deleting edge pixels whose demise will not change the connectivity of the image.

Algorithms are available which can also deal with three dimensional binary images, [Tsao and Fu 81] for example.

Contributor: Dave Reynolds.

Reference

[Tsao and Fu 81]
                Tsao, Y.F. and Fu, K.S.
                A Parallel Thinning Algorithm for 3-D Pictures.
                Computer Graphics and Image Processing 17:315-331, 1981.

235. SKOLEMIZATION

A technique borrowed from **mathematical logic** (and named after the mathematician Skolem), but much used in **automatic theorem proving**, for removing **quantifiers** from **predicate calculus** <189> formulae. If $A(y)$ is a formula with free variables y, x_1, ..., x_n, then $\forall y\ A(y)$ is replaced by $A(y)$, and $\exists y\ A(y)$ is replaced by $A(f(x_1, ..., x_n))$, where f is a new **Skolem function**. The technique is usually applied to formulae which have all their quantifiers at the front (**Prenex normal form**), but can be adapted to any formula. It produces a formula which has a model if and only if the original formula does.

Contributor: Alan Bundy.

Reference

[Chang and Lee 73]
                Chang, C. and Lee, R.C.
                Symbolic Logic and Mechanical Theorem Proving.
                Academic Press, 1973.

236. SMALLTALK

SmallTalk is a programming environment developed by members of the Learning Research Group at the Xerox Palo Alto Research Center. A number of editions of SmallTalk have emerged over the past few years, starting with SmallTalk-72, which appeared around 1976 [Goldberg and Kay 76], and culminating with SmallTalk-80, announced in Byte magazine [Byte, 1981]. The fundamental philosophy of SmallTalk is developed from **Simula** [Birtwistle et al 73], and although the different editions differ in syntax, all share the view of a programming system as a collection of (active) objects, communicating by **passing messages**. In addition, SmallTalk adopted Simula's "class" concept, and has extended and refined it considerably. The power of the SmallTalk system arises mainly from the modularity enforced by the packaging of declarative and procedural knowledge into individual objects. If the services of an object are required, for instance, to access the value of a certain location in an array, a message is sent to the object which owns the array from the object which is interested in accessing it. The message will specify all pertinent information regarding the request, and will generate a response which should contain the value of the requested location.

Contributor: Mark Drummond.

References

[Birtwistle, Dahl, Myhraug and Nygaard 73]
  Birtwistle, G., Dahl O-J., Myhraug, B. and Nygaard, N.
  Simula Begin.
  Philadelphia, Auerbach, 1973.

[Goldberg and Kay 76]
  SmallTalk-72 Instruction manual
  Xerox PARC technical report, 1976.

237. SPATIAL DIFFERENTIATION

A method for sharpening images. It is used to intensify edges and consists in subtracting the second derivative of a function from the function itself. Since an image is represented by discrete pixels, the derivative of the picture function at a pixel is approximated by the difference in intensity between adjacent pixels, and the higher order differences from the first-order ones. See also **edge detection** <65>, **high-emphasis filtering** <94>.

Contributor: Luis Jenkins.

Reference

(Cohen and Feigenbaum 82)
  Cohen, P. and Feigenbaum, E. (editors).
  The Handbook of Artificial Intelligence Vol. 3.
  Kaufmann, 1982.

238. SPATIAL FREQUENCY CHANNELS

Spatial frequency channels are systems sensitive to a limited range of spatial frequencies. In the human visual system these are considered to be a population of cells with similar tuning characteristics specifically sensitive to a restricted range of the **contrast sensitivity function** <44> envelope. See **bandpass filter** <16>.

Contributors: T P Pridmore, S R Pollard, S T Stenton.

Reference

[Wilson and Bergen 79]
          Wilson, H.R. and Bergen, J.R.
          A Fourier Mechanism Model for Spatial Vision.
          Vision Research 19: 19-32, 1979.

239. SPELLING CORRECTION

An essential requirement for serious natural language processing programs, though not strictly an AI technique.

A simple strategy, based on a letter-by-letter tree-structured dictionary, assumes that errors fall into the four types: (i) extra letter (ii) substituted letter (iii) omitted letter and (iv) reversed latter pair. Then at any point where a mismatch between input string and dictionary string occurs a new match can be tried by, respectively, (i) advancing the input string one letter (ii) advancing both strings together (iii) advancing the dictionary string, and (iv) advancing first one string and then the other.

This strategy is looking for letter position correspondence between the two strings: weaker strategies look merely for ordinal correspondence, and yet weaker for 'material' correspondence, i.e. just having the same letters. The simple strategy described does not take account of the number of errors per word. Generalising for this requires a string similarity measure. Such measures allow the use of non-literal word representations, e.g. hash coding, and of n-gram rather than single-letter based matching. Spelling correction may also use heuristics exploiting e.g. distinctive properties of the language ('u' after 'q' in English), those of the input device (optical character reader, human typist), and the choice of strategy may be influenced by the task e.g. whether a large lexicon is involved, whether a user should be consulted for a proposed correction, etc. In the limit, error detection and correction requires full language understanding.

Contributor: Karen Sparck Jones.

Reference

[Pollock 82]   Pollock, J.J.
                 Spelling error detection and correction by computer: some notes and
                     a bibliography.
                 Journal of Documentation 38: 282-291, 1982.

240. STATE SPACE

Alias: **search space, problem space.**

Many problems can be represented as an initial state, a goal state and a set of **operators** <164> that define operations to go to new states from a given state. The states that can be reached from the initial state by applying the rules in all possible ways define the state space. The problem is then to reach the goal state from the initial state. By this formulation almost any problem can be reduced to a search problem.

Contributor: Maarten van Someren.

Reference

(Barr and Feigenbaum 81)
    Barr, A. and Feigenbaum, E.A. (editors).
    The Handbook of Artificial Intelligence Vol. 1.
    Kaufmann, 1981.

241. STEREOPSIS

The process of recovering the 3D structure of a scene from two different views. The problem has two parts; the measurement of the disparity of corresponding points in the two images, and the interpretation of these disparity measurements to recover the range and orientation of the surfaces in the scene.   See **intrinsic images <105>** and **relaxation labelling <105>**.

Contributors: T P Pridmore, S R Pollard, S R Stenton.

Reference

[Mayhew 83]   Mayhew, J.E.W.
               Stereopsis.
               In Braddick and Sleigh (editor), *Physical and Biological Processing
                   of Images, .   ,* 1983.

242. STRUCTURED INDUCTION

Structured induction employs the same top-down problem decomposition as structured programming, combined with bottom-up implementation of the individual subproblems.   A given problem is split into relevant attributes, those attributes that are not directly codable are split again.   This decomposition process is repeated for each attribute that is not immediately codable until none is left, producing a hierarchical tree of subproblems whose leaf nodes are directly codable attributes. Inductive inference is then used to solve each of the subproblems from the bottom of this hierarchy to the top.   Each newly solved subproblem is given a meaningful name which is used in the next level up as a simple coded attribute.   This process is continued until there are no more subproblem hierarchy levels to ascend.   A top level procedure now exists that when run, calls the lower level subproblems and attributes in an order determined by the inductive procedures applied at each level of the bottom-up implementation.   This technique was developed at the Machine Intelligence Research Unit, University of Edinburgh as an aid to the generation of humanly understandable classification rules for use in expert systems.

Contributor: Alen Shapiro.

Reference

127

[Shapiro and Niblett 82]
Shapiro, A. and Niblett, R.B.
Automatic Induction of Classification Rules for a Chess End-Game.
In *Advances in Computer Chess*, 3, . Permagon, 1982.

243. SUBGOALING

Alias: **problem reduction**.

Many planning systems use a **backward search** of the space that is defined by the available operators. The goal is split into subgoals, and the system then recursively tries to satisfy those subgoals. A major problem with this method is that the subgoals may be interdependent. To achieve subgoal G1 it may be necessary to apply an operator that makes it impossible to achieve subgoal G2. See **Interactions between subgoals <102>**.

); the debugging is done by specialist procedure that recognize patterns of interactions between subgoals and suggest repairs. Another one is to have 'abstract plans' that is underconstrained and that are progressively refined as new information is obtained [Stefik 80a,b]; each step in the abstract plan performs some general operation which is eventually turned into an actual operation or possibly a set of operations.]

Contributor: Maarten van Someren.

References

[Nilsson 80]
Nilsson, N.J.
Principles of Artificial Intelligence.
Tioga Pub. Co., 1980.

[Stefik 80]
Stefik, M.J.
Planning with constraints (Molgen: part 1) and Planning and Meta-planning (Molgen: part2).
Artificial Intelligence 14, 1980.

[Sussman 75]
Sussman, G.J.
A computer model of skill acquisition.
Elsevier, 1975.

244. SYNICS

SYNICS is a translator writing system which uses a **top-down** table driven parser. The system is designed to be called from a main program passing to the subroutines the string to be translated and on return there will be the translation or an error message explaining why the translation did not take place. Input to the translator building system is in a form of BNF with the rules for the translation being associated with each of the production rules. There are some extensions to the normal BNF in that there is a 'not' option an 'if-then-else' construct and selective backup. There is also the facility to allow the user to call his own routine during both parsing and translation to make decisions at these points.

SYNICS 1.5 is a user interface management system incorporating all of the functions of SYNICS. In SYNICS 1.5, dialogue control is described by recursive transition networks.

The programs are written in Fortran IV and 77.

Contributor: Steve Guest.

Availability

Commercially available with documentation and support.   Special rates to academic institutions.

Environment: On Perq PNX, GEC 4000, VAX-VMS.

From: Professor E.A. Edmonds,
      Human-Computer Interface Research Unit,
      Leicester Polytechnic,
      P.O. Box 143,
      Leicester LE1 9BH,
      England.

      Electronic address: eflt50@ltga

245. TABLE OF MULTIPLE EFFECTS

This is a table relating patterns (representing facts) to nodes in a plan where they are asserted or denied.   It is used by **non-linear planners** <158> to detect quickly interferences between actions on parallel branches.   It is a simplified form of the **Goal Structure** <86> which holds more extensive information on the ranges for which conditions must be kept true to achieve their purpose.   However, it can also be used to recognise beneficial **side effects** which may allow other goals to be satisfied without introducing new actions.

Contributor: Austin Tate.

Reference

[Sacerdoti 77]   Sacerdoti, E. D.
                 AS Structure for plans and behaviour.
                 Elsevier North-Holland, New York, 1977.

246. TEMPLATE MATCHING

A simple technique that is sometimes used in language understanding.   A language unit (sentence or phrase) is compared with a set of predefined 'templates'. Some positions in the template consist of variables that match any input. If a template matches the input, the variables take the value of the corresponding elements in the input. Eg. the template "Var1 hits Var2" matches the input "Mary hits John with her hand" and Var1 takes the value "Mary" and Var2 "John with her hand".   Template matching is only useful if there is a small number of templates, otherwise the matching process is too expensive.

Contributor: Maarten van Someren.

Reference

(Barr and Feigenbaum 81)
        Barr, A. and Feigenbaum, E.A. (editors).
        The Handbook of Artificial Intelligence Vol. 1.
        Kaufmann, 1981.

247. TIME COMPLEXITY OF RECOGNITION

A measure of the computational complexity of recognising strings of a language characterised in a particular grammatical formalism.   Usually given as the worst-case asymptotic upper bound - that is, one proves how a particular recognition algorithm will perform on arbitrarily long strings of a language whose grammar is the worst possible for the given algorithm.   See also **Earleys Algorithm <64>**.

Contributor: Henry Thompson.

Reference

[Perrault 83]   Perrault, C.R.
        On the Mathematical Properties of Linguistic Theories.
        In *Proceedings of the 21st Annual Meeting of the Association for Computational Linguistics*.   Association for Computational Linguistics, Stanford, CA, 1983.

248. TOP-DOWN PARSING

Alias: **hypothesis-driven parsing**.

In trying to parse a string with a grammar, if one starts with the grammar and tries to fit it to the string, this is top-down parsing.   For instance with a **context-free grammar <41>**, one starts with expansions for the initial symbol, and builds down from there trying to find an expansion which will get to the symbols in the string.

Contributor: Henry Thompson.

Reference

[Winograd 83]   Winograd, T.
        Language as a cognitive process.
        Addison-Wesley, 1983.

249. T-PROLOG

T-PROLOG is a very high level simulation system which combines the time concept of discrete simulation languages and the non-procedural programming concepts of **PROLOG** <196>. It extends the traditional possibilities of simulation languages towards automatic problem solving by using explicit and implicit control of time and automatic model modification depending on logical deductions.

The interpreter can execute an arbitrary number of PROLOG-like goals in parallel, and if deadlock is reached further paths are explored by backtracking in time. The processes executing the goals can communicate through logical variables, through the database and by means of a **demon** <51> mechanism.

The current implementation of T-PROLOG is based on the **MPROLOG** <150> system and uses special built-in procedures for handling several pseudo-parallel threads of control.

Contributors: Steve Todd and Robert Corlett.

Availability

From: Dr Julia Sipka,
      Systems, Computers and Informatics Laboratory (SCIL),
      1011 Budapest,
      Iskola u.10,
      HUNGARY.

References

[Futo and Szeredi 82]
                    Futo,. I. and Szeredi, J.
                    A Discrete Simulation System Based on Artificial Intelligence Methods.
                    In *Discrete Simulation and Related Fields,* . North Holland, 1982.

[Szeredi and Santane-Toth 82]
                    Szeredi, P. and Santane-Toth, E.
                    Prolog Applications in Hungary.
                    In *Logic Programming,* . Academic Press, 1982.

250. TRUTH MAINTENANCE SYSTEM

A truth maintenance system (TMS) is used to record justifications for assertions. Such justifications can be used to generate explanations and to track down the assumptions underlying assertions. In **RUP** <219> every justification is a disjunctive clause of sentential (propositional) atoms and any such clause can be treated as a justification. RUP's TMS takes a set of such propositional clauses and performs propositional **constraint propagation** <39> to ensure that every assertion with a valid justification is in fact believed by the system (thus ensuring a deduction **invariant**). RUP's TMS also ensures that there is an entry on a contradiction queue for every propositional clause all of whose atoms are false.

Contributor: D. McAllester.

References

[Doyle 78]   Doyle, J.
                 Truth Maintenance Systems for Problem Solving.
                 Technical Report 419, MIT AI Lab, September, 1978.

[McAllester 80] McAllester, D.
                 An Outlook on Truth Maintenance.
                 Technical Report 551, MIT AI Lab, August, 1980.

251. TYPED PRECONDITIONS

In early problem solving systems (eg **STRIPS**) and planning languages (eg **PLANNER** <143>) the operators were given a single set of preconditions which were always interpreted as "test if true, or subgoal to make them true". The need to distinguish between the case in which the planner should only check if something was already true or should be allowed to add further actions into a plan to make the condition true was recognised as an important search control mechanism in **POPLER**. This led to two different types of precondition. Additions were also made to various pattern directed invocation systems which clustered alternative methods together and made a choice from them on the basis of some pre-occurring fact.

The utility of typed preconditions and their different properties for both hierarchic domain description and planner search space control was investigated in the **NONLIN** <158> planner which recognised 4 precondition types: SUPERVISED, UNSUPERVISED, USEWHEN and ACHIEVE.

Contributor: Austin Tate.

References

[Davies 73]   Davies, D. J. M.
                 POPLER 1.5 Reference Manual.
                 Technical Report, DAI, 1973.

[Tate 76]   Tate, A.
                 NONLIN: a hierarchic non-linear planning system.
                 Research Report 25, DAI, 1976.

252. UNIFICATION

A process, used in **resolution** <212>, for determining whether two expressions of the **predicate calculus** <189> will match. Terms of an expression in predicate calculus may be of one of three forms: **constant**, **variable** or **function**, where the last of these is made up of a function symbol applied to a number of terms. A **substitution** is a set of ordered pairs where the first element of each pair is a term and the second a variable. Applying such a substitution to a formula means that each variable appearing in the set of ordered pairs is replaced by the term which it is matched with in the substitution. Two expressions are unifiable if there is a substitution (the unifier) which when applied to both expressions makes them identical. A unification algorithm determines whether the given expressions are unifiable and, if so, finds a unifying substitution. It is usual in **resolution** based systems to specify that the substitution which is applied to unify two expressions is

132

the most general such substitution, thus the expressions lose as little generality as is necessary to make the resolution go through.

Contributor: Dave Plummer.

Reference

[Nilsson 80]   Nilsson, N. J.
                 Principles of Artificial Intelligence.
                 Tioga Pub. Co., 1980.

253. UNITS

The Units system is a frame-based interactive knowledge acquisition, representation and manipulation system. It was developed by Mark Stefik and others at Stanford University as part of the MOLGEN project and it has subsequently been used by several other projects. Knowledge is stored in "units" which may be divided into possibly overlapping partitions. Units have slots, and procedures may be attached to slots and units. These procedures may be written in LISP or a specially provided pseudo-English procedural language. There are built-in property inheritance mechanisms and pattern matchers, but most of the inference must be provided by application specific methods. The system also includes mechanisms for automatically documenting knowledge bases, for examining knowledge bases, and for transferring information within and among knowledge bases. (c.f. KRL <115>, FRL <78> and KL-ONE/KL-TWO <113>.)

Contributor: Robert Corlett.

Availability

From: Intelligenetics,
      124 University Avenue,
      Palo Alto,
      California 94301,
      USA.

Reference

[Stefik 79]   Stefik, M.
                 An Examination of a Frame-Structured Representation System.
                 In *Proceedings of IJCAI-79*, pages 845-852. International Joint
                 Conference on Artificial Intelligence, 1979.

254. THE UT THEOREM PROVER

The UT theorem prover is probably the best known natural deduction <153> theorem prover. It was written in LISP <34> by Woody Bledsoe and his co-workers at the University of Texas, and is best described in [Bledsoe and Tyson 75]. The theorem prover embodies a Gentzen-like deduction system for first-order predicate calculus, and many special purpose techniques, including: subgoaling, rewrite rules, controlled forward chaining, controlled definition instantiation, conditional procedures,

and induction.   The prover, though powerful in its own right, is essentially
interactive and thus allows the user of the prover to control the search for the proof
in radical ways.   The user can for example : add hypotheses, instruct the prover to
instantiate certain variables with values, or instruct the prover as to which deduction
rule to use next.

Contributor: Dave Plummer.

Reference

[Bledsoe and Tyson 75]
                Bledsoe, W.W. and Tyson, M.
                The UT interactive Prover.
                Memo ATP-17, Math. Dept., U. of Texas, May, 1975.

255. VARIABLE-VALUED LOGIC

Variable-valued logic is an extension of some known many-valued logics (MVL) in
two directions:

1. It permits the propositions and variables in the propositions to take
    values from different domains, which can vary in the kind and number of
    elements and also in the structure relating to the elements.

2. It generalises some of the traditionally used operators and adds new
    operators which are "most orthogonal" to the former.

Variable-valued logics have found applications in pattern recognition, medical
decision making, discrimination of structural textures.   These logics have been
successfully used in construction of diagnostic expert systems that can acquire
knowledge by **inductive learning** from examples.

Contributor: L.J. Kohout.

References

[Michalski 77]   Michalski, R.S.
                Variable-valued logic and its Application to Pattern Recognition and
                    Machine Learning.
                In *Computer Science and Multiple-Valued Logic: Theory and
                    Applications.*, .   North-Holland", 1977.

[Michalski and Chilansky 81]
                Michalski, R.S., and Chilansky, R.L.
                Knowledge Acquisition by Encoding Expert Rules Versus Computer
                    Induction from Examples: a Case Study Involving Soybean
                    Pathology.
                In *Fuzzy Reasoning and its Applications*, .   AcademicPress, 1981.

256. VERSION SPACE

A technique for **learning** concept rules from instances that are presented sequentially. Given a description language on which a partial generality ordering is defined, and a series of instances, a rule is found that can classify instances as belonging to a concept or not. The method consists of maintaining two boundary sets that are defined in terms of the generality ordering: (1) a maximally specific set of descriptions (instances that fit one of these descriptions or a more specific one are positive instances of the concept) and (2) a minimally general set (instances that don't fit those descriptions (or more specific ones) are negative instances of the concept). The space below the upper boundary, containing all possible rules, is called the version space. The method for maintaining the boundaries is:

- positive instance: new specific boundary consists of the descriptions that fit the set union of instances covered by the previous boundary and the new instance

- negative instance: new general boundary consists of the descriptions that fit the set covered by the previous boundary minus the new one.

This method is only useful if there exists an elegant representation for the boundary sets. See **focussing <72>**.

Contributor: Maarten van Someren.

Reference

[Mitchell, T. M. 82]
          Mitchell.
          Generalization as search.
          Artificial Intelligence 18:203–226, 1982.

257. VIEWER–CENTRED CO–ORDINATES

Objects described in viewer-centred co-ordinates, as opposed to **object-centred co-ordinates <161>**, are those described in terms of a co-ordinate frame centred on the viewer, i.e. the viewer is considered to form the origin of the system and axes are defined relative to the line of sight and the retina.

Contributors: T P Pridmore, S R Pollard, S P Stenton.

Reference

[Marr 82]   Marr, D.
               Vision.
               Freeman, 1982.

258. VOCODER REPRESENTATION

The **vocoder** representation characterizes the speech signal in terms of energy in a series of fixed frequency bands. This form of analysis has been used as a stage in **speech recognition**, and as a means of data compression in storing speech for later **resynthesis**.

Contributor: Steve Isard.

259. VOLE

A family of geometric modelling systems created at the University of Bath that use spatial decomposition methods to produce fast picture output with full hidden-surface removal. Input takes the form of a **constructive solid geometry** tree, and it is written in FORTRAN in a PDP minicomputer.

Contributor: Stephen Cameron.

Availability

From: Dr John Woodwark,
      Department of Engineering,
      University of Bath,
      England.

260. VOWEL QUADRILATERAL

Alias: **vowel analysis**.

Employs an 8-pole **linear predictive coding** <123> analysis to provide 9 vocal tract log area parameters which are mapped by a principal component transformation into a plane. The principal component coefficients are calculated off-line. Can provide a real-time display of vowel position; and a further rotational transformation gives close approximation to classical vowel quadrilateral.

Contributor: Geoff Bristow.

Reference

[Bristow and Fallside 78]
                Bristow, G.J. & Fallside, F.
                Computer display of vowel quadrilateral with real-time representation
                    of articulation.
                Electronics Letters 14:107-109, 1978.

261. ZERO-CROSSINGS

A point at which a mathematical function changes its sign, i.e. passes through zero. Technically a zero-crossing is defined as the intersection of the zero plane (z=0) with a surface (z=f(x,y)). Convolving a **grey-level image** <89> with a difference of **gaussians** operator and then finding zero crossings in the output is one way of looking for edge points. See **edge detection <65>**.

Contributors: T P Pridmore, S R Pollard, S T Stenton.

Reference

[Marr 82]   Marr, D.
                 Vision.
                 Freeman, 1982.

262. ZETALISP

A major dialect of **LISP <34>**, distinguished by

1. special LISP-oriented hardware;

2. mostly implemented in LISP;

3. attempt to integrate use of the display into the language; and

4. provision (and use in the system code) of the Flavors package to allow a **message-passing** style of programming.

Contributor: Bruce Anderson.

Availability

Commercially available with documentation and support by licensing the LISP machine hardware and software technology. Systems descended from ZetaLisp are available from Symbolics Inc., (U.K. distributor EAL), and Lisp Machines Inc.

Reference

[Weinleb and Moon 81]
                 Weinleb, D. and Moon, D.
                 LISP machine manual
                 MIT AI Lab., 1981.

263. ZMOB

ZMOB is a hardware architecture developed at the University of Maryland intended for artificial intelligence work. The system essentially consists of a ring of 256 Z80A microprocessors connected to a host computer (a DEC VAX-11) which communicates to each processor via a high speed 48 bit wide, 257 stage shift register called the "conveyor belt". Each processor has its own 64 kbytes of memory and so the processors do not share common global data, but may only communicate by message passing via the high speed bus.

Contributor: Robert Corlett.

Reference

[Rieger, Trigg and Bane 81]
Rieger, C., Trigg, R. and Bane, B.
ZMOB: A New Computing Engine For AI.
Technical Report TR-1028, Dept. of Computer Science, Univ. of
Maryland, 1981.

264. ZOG

ZOG is a general-purpose human-computer interface system that combines the features of a database system, word processing, and an operating system shell. The primary features of ZOG are: (1) an emphasis on menu-selection as the primary interface mode; (2) the use of the selection process for navigation in the database, editing the content and structure of the database, and interaction with programs; (3) an architecture that supports the implementation and growth of very large, distributed databases; and (4) rapid system response.

Contributor: Jack Jeffers.

Availability

Available with some documentation. Informally supported.

Environment: PERQ under POS

From: Jack Jeffers,
Code 1828,
David Taylor Navy Ship Research and Development Center,
Bethesda,
Maryland 20084,
USA.

Tel: (202) 227-1618
Electronic address: JJeffers@DTRC (Arpanet)

Reference

[Robertson, Newell and McCracken 81]
Robertson, G., Newell, A. and McCracken, D.
The ZOG approach to man-machine communication.
International Journal of Man-Machine Studies 14:461-488, 1981.

Index of Definitions

2 1/2-D sketch   <u>1</u>, 105

A* algorithm   <u>2</u>, 23
acls: analogue concept learning system   <u>3</u>
active edge   30
actors   <u>4</u>, 151
acyclic graph   59
add list   163, 164
adversary problems   15
AGE   <u>5</u>
agenda   19, 92, 140, 214
Agent   28
AL/X   <u>8</u>
ALGOL-60   125, 221
ALICE   <u>6</u>
alpha/beta pruning   <u>7</u>, 7, 15
alpha/beta search   15
AMORD   <u>9</u>
analogical problem solving   <u>10</u>
AND/OR tree   61
antecedent   38
antecedent theorem   51, 143
APES   <u>11</u>, 144
APL   156
applicative language   96
APT   160
ARBY   <u>12</u>
array   75
assertion interning   219
assertional database   196
assertions   203
associative database   143, <u>13</u>
ATN   14, 30
atomic sentence   33
audiogram   35
augmented transition network   <u>14</u>, 27, 109
automatic theorem proving   33, 22, 170, 212, 235
AUTOPASS   217
axioms   189

B* algorithm   <u>15</u>
backtracking parser   54
backward chaining   5, 8, 66, 68, 111, 220
backward search   243
bags   203
bandpass filter   <u>16</u>, 238
Bayesian inference   <u>17</u>, 142
best first search   15, 92
bidirectional search   <u>18</u>
binary image   87, 98
Binary Relationship model   224
blackboard   5, <u>19</u>, 91
BLISS-10   166
blocks world   110
bottom-up   20, 30, 76

148

150

Symbolic Computation

Managing Editors: **J. Encarnação, D. W. Loveland**

Artificial Intelligence

Editors: **L. Bolc, A. Bundy, P. Hayes, J. Siekmann**

Automation of Reasoning 1

Classical Papers on Computational Logic 1957–1966
Editors: **J. Siekmann, G. Wrightson**
1983. XII, 525 pages. ISBN 3-540-12043-2

Automation of Reasoning 2

Classical Papers on Computational Logic 1967–1970
Editors: **J. Siekmann, G. Wrightson**
1983. XII, 637 pages. ISBN 3-540-12044-0

Logic has emerged as one of the fundamental disciplines of computer science. Computational logic, which continues the tradition of logic in a new technological setting, has led to such diverse fields of application as automatic program verification, program synthesis, question answering systems, and deductive data bases as well as logic programming and the 5th generation computer system. These two volumes, the first covering the years 1957–1966 and the second, 1967–1970, contain those papers which shaped and influenced the field of computational logic. They make available the classical works in the field, which in many cases were difficult to obtain or had not previously appeared in English.

M. M. Botvinnik

Computers in Chess

Solving Inexact Search Problems

Translated from the Russian by A. A. Brown
With contributions by A. J. Reznitsky, B. M. Stilman,
M. A. Tsfasman, A. D. Yudin
1984. 48 figures. XIV, 158 pages. ISBN 3-540-90869-2

Contents: The General Statement. – Methods for Limiting the Search Tree. – The Search for a Solution and Historical Experience. – An Example of the Solution of an Inexact Problem (Chess). – Three Endgame Studies (An Experiment). – The Second World Championship. – Appendix 1: Fields of Play. – Appendix 2: The Positional Estimate and Assignment of Priorities. – Appendix 3: The Endgame Library in PIONEER (Using Historical Experience by the Handbook Method and the Outreach Method). – Appendix 4: An Associative Library of Fragments. – References. – Glossary of Terms. – Index of Notation. – Index.

Springer-Verlag
Berlin
Heidelberg
New York
Tokyo

Machine Learning

An Artificial Intelligence Approach

Editors: **R. S. Michalski, J. G. Carbonell, T. M. Mitchell**
With contributions by numerous experts

1984. XI, 572 pages
(Symbolic Computation. Artificial Intelligence)
ISBN 3-540-13298-8
(Originally published by Tioga Publishing Company, 1983)

Contents: General Issues in Machine Learning. – Learning from Examples. – Learning in Problem-Solving and Planning. – Learning from Observation and Discovery. – Learning from Instruction. – Applied Learning Systems. – Comprehensive Bibliography of Machine Learning. – Glossary of Selected Terms in Machine Learning. – About the Authors. – Author Index. – Subject Index.

N. J. Nilsson

Principles of Artificial Intelligence

1982. 139 figures. XV, 476 pages
(Symbolic Computation. Artificial Intelligence)
ISBN 3-540-11340-1
(Originally published by Tioga Publishing Company, 1980)
(Available in North America through William Kaufmann, Inc.)

Contents: Prologue. – Production Systems and AI. – Search Strategies for AI Production Systems. – Search Strategies for Decomposable Production Systems. – The Predicate Calculus in AI. – Resolution Refutation Systems. – Rule-Based Deduction Systems. – Basic-Plan-Generating Systems. – Advanced Plan-Generating Systems. – Structured Object Representations. – Prospectus. – Bibliography. – Author Index. – Subject Index.

Springer-Verlag
Berlin
Heidelberg
New York
Tokyo